ART, CREATIVITY, LIVING

Winnicott Studies Monograph Series

The Person Who Is Me:
Contemporary Perspectives on the True and False Self
edited by Val Richards

Fathers, Families, and the Outside World
edited by Val Richards

André Green at The *Squiggle* Foundation
edited by Jan Abram

The *Squiggle* Foundation is a registered charity
set up in 1981 to study and cultivate the tradition
of D. W. Winnicott. For further information, contact
The Administrator, 33 Amberley Road, London N13 4BH.
Tel: 020 8882 9744; Fax: 020 8886 2418

Winnicott Studies Monograph Series

ART, CREATIVITY, LIVING

edited by

Lesley Caldwell

London & New York
KARNAC BOOKS
for
The *Squiggle* Foundation

W. H. Auden, "To Unravel Unhappiness", in *The Complete Works of W. H. Auden, Vol. I: Prose 1926–1938*, ed. E. Mendelson (London: Faber & Faber, 1993), reproduced by permission of the publisher.

Extracts from R. M. Rilke, *Selected Works, Vol. 2: Poetry*, trans. J. B. Leishman (London: Hogarth Press, 1960), reproduced by permission of the publisher.

D. W. Winnicott, "Critical Notice of *On Not Being Able to Paint*", reproduced by arrangement with Mark Paterson and Associates on behalf of the Winnicott Trust, London.

First published in 2000 by
H. Karnac (Books) Ltd., 58 Gloucester Road, London SW7 4QY

A subsidiary of Other Press LLC, New York

British Library Cataloguing in Publication Data

A C.I.P. for this book is available from the British Library

ISBN 1 85575 253 0

10 9 8 7 6 5 4 3 2 1

Edited, designed, and produced by Communication Crafts

Printed in Great Britain by Polestar Wheatons Ltd, Exeter

www.karnacbooks.com

Dedicated to Marion Milner [1900–1999]

CONTENTS

CONTRIBUTORS

W. H. AUDEN [1907–1973] was born in York and educated at Christ Church, Oxford. From the publication of his first collection of verse in 1928 he became recognized as one of the leading poets of the twentieth century. He also wrote opera libretti, criticism, and drama. The essay reproduced in this volume is taken from Auden's *Prose 1926–1938*, published by Faber & Faber and edited by his literary executor, Edward Mendelson.

VINCENZO BONAMINIO teaches Dynamic Psychopathology and Child Psychotherapy in the Department of Child and Adolescent Psychiatry at the University of Rome, "La Sapienza". He is a practising psychoanalyst (adult and child) and a full member of the Italian Psychoanalytic Society. He also teaches on the training course in Child and Adolescent Psychoanalytic Psychotherapy of A.S.N.E-S.I.Ps.I.A, Rome, and is currently its Director. He is on the editorial board of the journal *Richard e Piggle*.

MALCOLM BOWIE is Marshal Foch Professor of French Literature in the University of Oxford and a Fellow of All Souls. He is the author of *Freud Proust Lacan: Theory as Fiction* (1987), *Lacan* (1991), *Psychoanalysis and the Future of Theory* (1993), *Proust Among the Stars* (1998).

LESLEY CALDWELL is the Director of the *Squiggle* Foundation and the Editor of *Winnicott Studies*. She is Senior Lecturer at the University of Greenwich and a Psychoanalytic Psychotherapist in private practice. She is the author of *Italian Family Matters* (1991) and editor of *Psychoanalysis and Culture* (1995), and she also writes on Italian cinema.

MARIASSUNTA DI RENZO has worked for more than twenty years as a psychologist and child psychotherapist in the Department of Child and Adolescent Psychiatry at the University of Rome, "La Sapienza". She is a practising psychoanalyst (child and adult) and a member of the Italian Psychoanalytic Society. She also teaches on the training course in Child and Adolescent Psychoanalytic Psychotherapy, A.S.N.E-S.I.Ps.I.A., Rome

JOHN FIELDING is Senior Academic at the Lycée Français Charles de Gaulle, where he teaches English. He was, with Alexander Newman, a founder editor of *Winnicott Studies*. He is interested in Shakespeare and the overlap between literature and psychoanalysis.

ADAM PHILLIPS is a child psychotherapist in private practice and a Patron of the *Squiggle* Foundation. His latest book is *Darwin's Worms* (1999).

MICHAEL PODRO is Emeritus Professor, University of Essex, a Fellow of the British Academy, and a Patron of the *Squiggle* Foundation. His books include *The Critical Historians of Art* (1982) and *Depiction* (1998).

MARGARET WALTERS is a writer and broadcaster.

DONALD WINNICOTT [1896–1971] was trained in paediatrics before training as a psychoanalyst. He continued both professions until his death. He became a member of the British Psycho-Analytical Society in 1935 and was twice its president. Among his publications are *Through Paediatrics to Psychoanalysis* (1958) and *The Maturational Processes and the Facilitating Environment* (1965).

KEN WRIGHT is a psychoanalyst and psychiatrist in private practice. He trained with the Independent group of the British Psycho-Analytical Society and at the Tavistock Clinic and Maudsley Hospital. He is the author of *Vision and Separation—Between Mother and Baby* (1991), which won the 1992 Mahler Literature prize. He is particularly influenced by Winnicott; his interests include the development and use of symbols and the relationship between creativity and the life of the self. He is a Patron of the *Squiggle* Foundation.

ART, CREATIVITY, LIVING

Introduction

Continuities in art and psychoanalysis

Lesley Caldwell

Writing in *The Listener* in 1934, Auden described Marion Milner's first book, *A Life of One's Own* (1934), written under the pseudonym Joanna Field, as an attempt "to chart ordinary unhappiness", "a remarkable and important book". The book preceded Milner's training as an analyst, and it is precisely this non-specialist ordinariness, which is not ordinary at all, that he applauds. Her clear exposition of the gap between her accepted sense of herself and the person she discovers herself to be through a kind of self-analysis mirrors the Freudian account of how we are constituted by processes of which we are unaware. Auden [chapter seven] reads approvingly Milner's insistence that this can be not only a dismaying but an exhilarating process. Two aspects he singles out remained central throughout Milner's long life: "that the expression of thought in words, becoming aware of it, was the beginning of a process of development and enrichment . . . and that the unconscious is . . . a source of creative wisdom; there is an instinctive sense of living, if it is trusted; a trust, however, quite different from blind irrationalism." Milner's interest in the positive aspects of symbolism and the value and necessity of illusion inform a clinical practice that always stressed the potential freedom to explore offered by and within the boundaries of the session. This is returned to, directly or indirectly, by other contributors to this volume as part of the more general questions that reading Milner encourages: why art matters, and, more especially, why and how art matters to psychoanalysis. The ongoing work and, it could be said, play of the mind in a series of real and imaginary engagements with others makes for a sort of continuum between the work of the figure Freud called the "creative artist", the work of the consulting-room, the responses of the audience for art works, and the capacity for satisfactions in ordinary lives that also depends on the almost infinite potential for creating new objects (Green, 1997, p. 1083). On the other hand, there are also differences in these forms of work, play, and creative living, and the papers collected here pursue those differences through what happens in the spaces of the consulting-room and the relationship of clinician and analysand lived out there [Bonaminio & Di Renzo]; through the mapping of the artist's engagement with his/her chosen medium and the early experiences of the baby [Wright]; through the meeting place established in the triangular relationships set up between text, artist, and reader/viewer; and through the commitment to engaging with what particular texts have to offer [Podro, Phillips, Bowie, Fielding]. These experiences and their different settings all engage an intermediate meeting place—the transitional space—where a quality of experience offered can add substantially, for those who can use it, to the pleasures of both satisfaction and consolation that living can hold. It is the creation and use of the concept of transitional space that distinguishes Donald Winnicott's contribution to the discussion of psychoanalytic technique, to the work of the artist, and to living as a creative activity available to all.

In his 1952 review of *On Not Being Able to Paint*, which Marion Milner wrote under the pseudonym Joanna Field, Winnicott [chapter eight] identifies illusion and spontaneity as aspects of the "subjective way of experiencing" that are found in both the intimate satisfactions and intensities offered by art, and also in unremarkable aspects of living. Both Winnicott and Milner place the origins of creativity in a period that precedes the individual's perceived need for reparation, a more fundamental experience, belonging to an earlier stage of emotional development. In this period, maternal care and empathy facilitate the conditions for the development of infant ego organization and the establishment of a self made possible only through the guarantee of a continuity of being derived from the mother–baby couple. Winnicott describes painting as Milner's "jumping-off place" for thinking about the subjective role of experiencing and for establishing a link between it and what is traditionally thought of as the sublimatory activity of the artist, but is here extended to offer a very different account: "wish-fulfilling illusion may be the essential basis for all true objectivity . . . a psychic reality for which the word illusion is inappropriate."

"It is life which crystallizes the first objects to which desire attaches itself, before even thought can cling to them" (Laplanche, 1976, p. 126). Thus Laplanche completes his brilliant account of the alternately speculative and scientistic *Beyond the Pleasure Principle* (Freud, 1920g), from which he particularly identifies the obsessional drive of the Freudian texts, under the necessity of the Oedipus complex. Laplanche argues that the repetitions that shape both its form and its argument are read as aspects of Freud's own passionate attachments, which infuse his accounts, offering rewards extending well beyond their presentation of mental models accounting for sublimatory activities. And in *Civilization and Its Discontents* (1930a) Freud himself emerges as decidedly ambivalent about the respective weighting of loss and gain in the civilizing process, in the pursuit of libidinal gratification or the differently insistent claims of the pleasures of the art object.

What psychoanalysis has done with art and with artists, through its concern with the cultural artefact as a symptom whose neurotic origins may be delivered up through a kind of content analysis, is one area to which many of the contributors to this volume return in their own different kinds of interest in the irreducibility of the art object and the compelling nature of the pleasures it offers: its illumination of the everyday, its extension of what is to be experienced, known, and endured of life and living, its insistent link with activities whose affirmation is the affirmation not only of the best of living and of human endeavour, but of the place of human aggression and destructiveness. The separation and combination of subjective and objective experience that is a taken-for-granted part of ordinary living is returned to when the authors highlight art, clinical practice, and living as facilitating the convergence of personal trajectories that are always also social. Like psychoanalysis, art is a relational activity, and Winnicott is consistently returned to as the basis for a different kind of thought and thinking. Malcolm Bowie [chapter one] describes Winnicott as offering simultaneously a more modest and a more innovative approach to culture than that to be derived from Freud's extensive interest in literature and the reciprocal relationship of psychoanalysis and literature embedded in the very literariness of Freud's own texts. In these articles it is through the centrality that Winnicott ascribes to play and to the complexity of the concept of transitional phenomena that infantile experience and artistic activity may be linked. Reading him in conjunction with three other twentieth-century authors—Rilke, Proust, and Woolf—Bowie illuminates the work of all four. Adam Phillips [chapter two] starts from the preoccupation of psychoanalysis with Shakespeare and with *Hamlet* and then fashions a set of questions about Freud and wonders about the kind of knowledge that psychoanalysis makes available as a set of statements about the business of being human. Again, it is Winnicott who, by exercising a kind of freedom in his plundering of others' accounts of the play, produces the really interesting questions about it—his identification of Hamlet's concern, "to be or not to be", with his own interest in being and doing. These terms—so frequently and stereotypically associated with femininity and masculinity and, as such, hampering in their potential to encourage thought—are here offered, through an interrogation of Hamlet himself, as a starting point for Phillips's own preliminary interrogation of those very terms.

Shakespeare is also the basis of John Fielding's discussion [chapter three] of *Othello*, though with an emphasis on the importance of words and language as the foundational tools of the talking cure. In a close study of the recognition in the last act of the play by Emilia, Desdemona's maid and Iago's wife, of how much knowledge of the components of the tragedy had always been available to her, Fielding draws on Bollas's suggestive description "the unthought known" and on Winnicott's interest in intermediate states as aids to his reading of the play and his enquiry into the status of knowing and not knowing in Shakespeare, and in the analytic session. In elaborating the continuities and the differences between the analytic and the literary text, these writers offer concrete examples of the parallels between them.

Michael Podro [chapter four] takes a statement of Milner's about the differential importance accorded to an art work by the analyst of the artist and by the artist him/herself, to ask how it is that painters can endow the canvas with form in such a way as simultaneously to pursue a personal interest and to provide for the participation of others. In Rembrandt's self-portraits, Podro identifies as central the interplay of artist as artist and artist as person, and its replication of the "doubleness" on which the activity of engaging with a painting depends. The activation of the set of mental activities on the part of the viewer that depend on recognition and imagining, on the meeting of subjective and objective, in the activity of looking, occurs through the combined skills and knowledge of both artist and viewer. Podro takes his distance from the interpretations of paintings as biography, while also cautioning against a total disregard for the facts of the life of the artist. Instead, he stresses how representation, technique, and life itself combine to symbolize a new object whose participation in all these registers offers a particular meeting place that can be used by both artist and viewer. Podro addresses briefly the two dominant Freudian insights from *Jokes and Their Relation to the Unconscious* (1905c) and the *Three Essays* (1905d) to make a closer link with Winnicott's interest in the baby's uttering or seeking a response. For Podro, then, the mother–baby dialogue becomes not an analogue of the painter and viewer but of how the painting itself offers the space for the use of initial recognitions. There is a link here with Ken Wright's chapter [chapter five] and its emphasis on the art object as "an object transformed by [the artist's] subjectivity". Wright locates creativity in the Winnicottian account of the self, but he further extends it with ideas of attunement drawn from Daniel Stern to argue for the artist's creation of self and world, of inside and outside, through a capacity—which may also be a necessity—to make forms that fit experience. Wright argues for Winnicott's account of creativity as also a care of the self, proposing that the baby's creative act in transforming the bit of blanket into a transitional object has relevance for the artist's own activity and its grounding in unconscious associations of maternal recognition.

In the only directly clinical contribution in this volume, Bonaminio and Di Renzo [chapter six] draw extensively on Milner for their own description of the continuities between play, dreaming, and the analytic session. They describe some extracts from the analyses of three children whose development of a particular sense of self emerges from the ongoing work of their sessions and the analysts' decisions to allow the space forged in the consulting-room to be a space for the child's exploration, alone, of parts of the self that had not previously been available for use. This work employs a literary text, *Alice in Wonderland,* session material, a dream, and the analysts' own thoughts to argue for the usefulness, clinically, of the style of Milner and Winnicott, with its emphasis upon the connections between subjective and objective and the positive evaluation of the illusion—which is not only an illusion—of oneness in the mind.

In his paper, "The Location of Cultural Experience" (1967), Winnicott says,

> it interests me however, as a side issue, that in any cultural field it is not possible to be original except on a basis of tradition. Conversely no one in the line of cultural contributors repeats, except as deliberate quotation, and the unforgivable sin in the cultural field is plagiarism; the interplay between originality and the acceptance of tradition as the basis for inventiveness seems to me to be just one more example and a very exciting one, of the interplay of separateness and union. . . . In using the word culture I am thinking of the inherited tradition, I am thinking of something that is in the common pool of humanity into which individuals and groups may contribute and from which we all draw if we have somewhere to put what we find. [p. 99]

Two interrelated arenas here offer insights into the creative process. First, the value of knowing and experiencing something at first hand: how knowing of that kind depends upon knowing the field, and how to know the field means to make use of it. That is, there is somewhere to "put" an experience and its pulling together of external and internal, the more that art, as a phenomenon of the in-between, can provide something fundamental. The encounter with an artefact is deepened by knowledge of it, of the specificity of the process of artistic creation, of the conventions, constraints, and particularities of the particular medium, of the tradition of work, and of the explorations internal to it. Knowledge and familiarity provide the place for artist and viewer to put the symbolic object that engages the creativity of both participants. Second, the more recognition there is of the dependence of one's own involvement with the work of others, both individually and as a field of work, the more there is something to be found and used in its turn. Phillips finds Winnicott's use of *Hamlet* not just different, but more provoking of thought and pleasure on the part of a reader; but this originality resides in Winnicott's imaginative use of others' readings.

The ruthlessness of the artistic enterprise and its dependence on others has been admirably described by the Italian film director, Gianni Amelio. In 1976, the then 31-year-old Amelio, who despite a lengthy apprenticeship as an assistant director was still at the beginning of his career, made a documentary for Italian television on the making of *1900*, Bernardo Bertolucci's sixth film. *Bertolucci secondo il cinema,* a titular emphasis that reverses the usual formula for documentaries of this kind—"the cinema according to . . ."—is, said Amelio, an exploration of a "cinematic father". But it is Amelio's description, twenty years later, of what he was doing that echoes Winnicott's description of originality as necessarily implicated in the ruthless use of what others have produced.

> Bertolucci according to the cinema is envy in sixteen mill, envy of thirty-five mill, envy of Bernardo's set. . . . What was I doing? I was trying to "challenge" Bertolucci in an absurd business, re-making what he did in one scene after another, trying to take it from different angles and so on. One critic gave the best definition of it, a film of plunder. . . . [But] what it gave me was the opportunity to follow closely a director for whom I had, and have, an enormous admiration while he worked on one of the incredibly rare Italian blockbusters. Not a Fellini or a Visconti, but someone sufficiently close in age who was on a wavelength that meant something to me too. . . . A rare opportunity for me to follow closely a film that had a year's production schedule and a million pound budget, and I exploited it to steal what I felt like taking from Bertolucci. In the cinema it's a good rule to go on stealing until you stop making films. I got very interested in the rehearsals with the actors of the scenes I

> knew so well from the screenplay. It was a theoretical exercise, and, even then I knew being a director involved more than retaking shots from a different angle; above all, it's about the preparing, about setting up the elements to put in front of the camera. The material here was Bertolucci's. I tried to understand how he did it, how he invented it. I think I was profoundly influenced by it, by the best things and the more dubious ones, and I still feel that influence now. [Amelio, 1995, p. 100]

Such a frank and moving account of an artistic relationship also depended upon Bertolucci's willingness to be used: a robbery, but also a homage—if one that does nothing to disguise the ruthless appropriation of the other's talents on which it is based. One corollary of the Oedipus complex for Johnathan Lear (1990)—one, moreover, it might be surmised, both Amelio and Winnicott would have endorsed—is that creativity requires that one come to grips with the legacies of one's intellectual parents, the challenge, pleasurable and non-pleasurable, of the past, and the potential it offers in the present. Amelio's determination links his own development to his use of the work of an admired cinematic father, but Bertolucci's agreement has parallels with the role of the mother in the infant's early process of separating and establishing the bases for individuation in the growing recognition of what belongs to the other and what belongs to the self.

"I suggest that creativity is one of the common denominators of men and women; in another language however, creativity is the prerogative of women. In yet another language it is a masculine feature" (Winnicott, 1989, p. 169). Margaret Walters' account [chapter nine] of her meeting with Marion Milner, first through her writing and then in person, stresses what Winnicott might call "the male and female elements" in Milner's personality and her abiding interest in the examination, in herself and in her writing, of a kind of femininity that is the prerogative of a certain kind of woman. Together with the short contributions [chapter ten] to the final plenary of the conference held by the *Squiggle* Foundation to honour Milner's work, at which the chapter by Michael Podro was also presented, Walters conveys a distinct personal intensity in her readings of the books, her descriptions of their author, and her own friendship with her. "Creativity is then the doing that arises out of being" (Winnicott, 1970, p. 40). From Walters and from all the contributors, Marion Milner's own intense participation in "the doing that arises out of being", whether in the consulting-room, in literary or artistic activity, or in her encounters with friends and colleagues, is recorded in the hope that it, too, will be used and reused by others.

CHAPTER ONE

Psychoanalysis and art: the Winnicott legacy

Malcolm Bowie

At first glance, Winnicott may seem to have a good deal less than, say, Freud or Lacan to offer students and practitioners of literary art. Freud and Lacan wrote at great and glorious length about the powers of language, each provided conceptual models in terms of which the modes of meaning characteristic of literary language in particular could be discussed, each was a rhetorician of the unconscious and a dramatist of the transferential encounter, and each was a powerfully original and complex writer. "Set a thief to catch a thief" is an appropriate workaday slogan in thinking about this relationship: if psychoanalysis is to become an instrument for the analysis of literature, let it face up squarely to its own character as a sequence of literary works and textual effects. Let Freud and Lacan help us to read literature, but also and simultaneously let us call upon literature to help us read Freud and Lacan. One has only to remember the uses to which Shakespeare's *Hamlet* and quotations from Goethe, Schiller, and Heine are put in *The Interpretation of Dreams* (Freud, 1900a), or the elaborate allegory of the psychoanalytic encounter that Lacan derives from his reading of Edgar Allan Poe's *The Purloined Letter*, to see how deep the complicity lies between certain kinds of psychoanalytic theory and certain kinds of creative writing.

Winnicott, on the other hand, offers few of these inducements to anyone visiting psychoanalysis from the field of literary studies. It is clear from many of his writings that he enjoys literature, painting, and music, but he seldom seeks to enlist them as corroborative evidence either in his theoretical papers or in his case studies. He writes well, but plainly and without conceit. He writes tentatively, in the manner of one who has tips and suggestions to offer his colleagues, rather than paradigms or doctrines: his rhetoric is one of collaboration between co-equals rather than one of solitary exertion and insight. In writing up his case histories, he attends primarily not to the verbal medium itself in which the dealings between analyst and analysand occur, but to the whole behavioural pattern of their interaction and to the part-real and part-fantasized space and time in which this interaction unfolds. He does not preen himself on his interpretative prowess. He lets his child patients play with their toys. He lets his adult patients re-enter a space of play, and toy with words, with the accidental accoutrements of the consulting-room, and with human time as it passes.

"Play is always exciting", Winnicott said in a talk on "Playing and Culture" given to the Imago Group in March 1968, adding, in a tone of voice that is itself a Winnicott fingerprint:

> It is exciting not because of the background of instinct, but because of the precariousness that is inherent in it, since it always deals with the knife-edge between the subjective and that which is objectively perceived. What holds for play also holds for the St. Matthew Passion at which I am almost certain to find colleagues when I go to the Festival Hall in a few week's time. [1968a, pp. 205–206]

Winnicott is content to leave Bach's great work on the margins of his own theory, to note a link between the play situation proper and the play of the artistic imagination and to leave matters there. It would not have seemed appropriate to him to bring the art work back into the world of theoretical reflection and treat it either as an allegory of the analytic dialogue or as a species of higher-order case material on which his very considerable powers of interpretation could go to work. Such things would have seemed to him grandiose and likely to distract the practitioner from the often humdrum clinical business in hand. Although Winnicott's ideas are perfectly extendable into the cultural sphere, as I shall seek to show in what follows, he did not himself extend them very far in that direction. Despite this self-denying ordinance on Winnicott's part, there are intellectual riches in his work for anyone who thinks about art, whether as an artist, a critic, a theorist, or a cultural commentator, and a power of provocation in them too. He takes us back to the great questions "What is art?" and "Why does art matter?" and he does so as a natural dramatist, as a watchful and wise inhabitant of "the knife-edge between the subjective and that which is objectively perceived".

Before going any further, we should remind ourselves of the complex content that Winnicott gave to the concept of "transitional phenomena", and of the enlarged range of meanings that he ascribed to the notion of "play". In order to do this convincingly in a short space, we cannot do better than reread these famous and richly implying paragraphs, which occur near the start of his paper on "Transitional Objects and Transitional Phenomena" (1951):

> I have introduced the terms "transitional object" and "transitional" phenomena for designation of the intermediate area of experience, between the thumb and the teddy bear, between the oral erotism and true object relationship, between primary creative activity and projection of what has already been introjected, between primary unawareness of indebtedness and the acknowledgement of indebtedness ("Say: ta!"). [p. 230]

By this definition an infant's babbling or the way an older child goes over a repertoire of songs and tunes while preparing for sleep come within the intermediate area as transitional phenomena, along with the use made of objects that are not part of the infant's body yet are not fully recognized as belonging to external reality.

It is generally acknowledged that a statement of human nature is inadequate when given in terms of interpersonal relationships, even when the imaginative elaboration of function, the whole of fantasy both conscious and unconscious, including the repressed unconscious, is allowed for. There is another way of describing persons, which comes out of the researches of the past two decades, that suggests that of every individual who has reached the stage of being a unit (with a limiting membrane and an outside and an inside) it can be said that there is an inner reality to that individual, an inner world that can be rich or poor and can be at peace or in a state of war.

My claim is that if there is a need for this double statement, there is a need for a triple one: there is the third part of the life of a human being, a part that we cannot ignore, an intermediate area of experiencing, to which inner reality and external life both contribute. It is an area that is not challenged, because no claim is made on its behalf except that it shall exist as a resting place for the individual engaged in the perpetual human task of keeping inner and outer reality separate yet inter-related.

It is usual to refer to "reality-testing" and to make a clear distinction between apperception and perception. I am here staking a claim for an intermediate state between a baby's inability and growing ability to recognize and accept reality. I am therefore studying the substance of illusion—that which is allowed to the infant and which, in adult life, is inherent in art and religion (Winnicott, 1975, p. 230).

This is worded with characteristic modesty, but we notice at once how radical a revision of one standard Freudian way at looking at things this is. Rather than think of the unconscious as irrupting into the operations of consciousness and as thereby creating interference patterns in the life of the individual, and rather than think of the return, under appropriate conditions, of repressed materials as being in itself therapeutic, as making a past pain liveable within the present, Winnicott directs our attention to an intermediate zone which is full of promise and danger, and to two realms that border that zone and are "separate yet interrelated". He opens up a potential space between inner and outer and seems often to think of this as the privileged site for psychoanalytic thinking and treatment.

The task of psychoanalysis is to allow the individual to inhabit this transitional or intermediate area without rushing to judgement by seeking premature emotional or intellectual certainties. In practical terms, this meant that the analyst should set great store by his own, and his patient's, toleration of antagonism and undecidability. In the talk on "Playing and Culture", which I have already quoted, Winnicott says:

> Undoubtedly the concept of the transitional object and of transitional phenomena brought me to wish to study this intermediate area which is neither dream nor object-relating. At the same time that it is neither the one nor the other of these two it is also both. This is the essential paradox . . . and we need to accept the paradox, not to resolve it. [1968a, p. 204]

"For me the paradox is inherent", he goes on to say. "Aetiologically," he insists within a few sentences, "the paradox must be accepted, not resolved." Winnicott's insistence and repetition in this paper and elsewhere are those of one who is conscious that what he is urging is both exciting and bothersome and runs against the grain of much previous psychoanalytic explanation. The space of potentiality which he opens up in these papers is multidimensional and mobile; it is the time-bound space of living human experience and needs to be protected against theories and analytic practices that would flatten, regularize, and normalize it by removing its paradoxical core.

The extraordinary thing about Winnicott's account of play is that it connects the world of infantile experience with the world of sophisticated cultural production in a way that, although modestly phrased, is in fact radical and far-reaching. "In order to give a place to playing I postulated a potential space between the baby and the mother", he wrote in "Playing: A Theoretical Statement" (1971b, p. 47). This space was adjacent to, and drew its energy from, what Winnicott had termed "primary psychic creativity" (1953, p. 34). This creativity, to which he paid tribute on a number of occasions, was the element that differentiated his views on the earliest stages of infant development from those of Klein and Fairbairn. Later forms of playfulness found their earliest prototype in a play of mind, a shape-changing capacity, a relish for antagonism, a future-directed, speculative power of invention, that seem to belong to infant experience from the beginning. But if Winnicott's "potential space" looks back to the primitive condition of minds, it looks forward too to minds in their most elaborately cultivated forms. "It is play that is the universal . . . the natural thing is playing" (1971b, p. 48). Psychoanalysis itself is "a highly specialized form of playing in the service of communication with oneself and others" (p. 48). What could be claimed for psychoanalysis—that it was a highly sophisticated form of something that belonged first of all to childhood—could be claimed for artistic activity too. What could be claimed for the mother–baby relationship—that it involved a perpetual "to and fro" (p. 55), a lasting playground of in-betweenness—could be claimed also for the art work in production and for the art work being read, or looked at, or heard. At both ends of the individual age spectrum, Winnicott takes his distance from Freud's own teaching, placing a seemingly un-Freudian emphasis both on a pre-sexual creativity in children and on the independent dignity, as it were, of cultural experience.

Paying tribute to the newly completed *Standard Edition* of Freud's works in 1966, Winnicott said:

> Freud did not have a place in his topography of the mind for things cultural. He gave new value to inner psychic reality, and from this came a new value for things that are actual and truly external. Freud used the word "sublimation" to point the way to a place where cultural experience is meaningful, but perhaps he did not get so far as to tell us where in the mind cultural experience is. [1967, p. 95]

Winnicott himself, on the other hand, does tell us "where in the mind cultural experience is", or rather he tells us that it is both in the mind and not in the mind, in a dangerous and thrilling border territory. The work of art belongs in no man's land, in the realm of push and pull, to and fro; it reaches towards the complex, the subtle-minded, integration of divergent and heterogeneous raw materials yet reaches backwards, too, to something primordial and pre-sexual. As Winnicott said in a celebrated footnote to his "Primitive Emotional Development" (1945): "Through artistic expression we can hope to keep in touch with our primitive selves whence the most intense feelings and even fearfully acute sensations derive, and we are poor indeed if we are only sane" (1975, p. 150). The work of art, well made in accordance with this prescription, would inhabit a supremely paradoxical locale: it would represent a triumph for the integrative and reparative capacities of the creative mind, yet at the same time take us to the threshold of a necessary madness; it would be the instrument both of closure and of a fearful new openness; it would take us back into the remote past and forward, defiantly, into a new future. Cultural experience would find its place, at last, within the psychoanalytic view of things, in restlessness, mobility, and an unceasing passage between fear and joy.

In what follows I shall test these propositions against a number of real works of art, and not just against their general effect, or the benign all-purpose phenomenology of artistic experience to which they might be thought to conduce, but against their local textures and the traces of the artist's labour that his or her works still bear. I shall suggest that Winnicott's account of creativity has much to tell us not simply about the uses to which we put artistic objects, but about the workshop practices amid which such objects are born. I shall speak about writers for the most part, and in particular about three great European writers belonging to the generation immediately before Winnicott's own: Rilke, born in 1875, Virginia Woolf, born in 1882, and Proust, born in 1871.

In talking about Rilke first of all, my cue comes from Winnicott himself, and from Clare Winnicott (1989), who begins her memoir "D.W.W.: A Reflection" (p. 1) with a quotation from Rilke's fourth Duino Elegy. Here the poet speaks of being *"im Zwischenraume zwischen Welt und Spielzeug"* [within a gap left between world and toy]. In one of the sequence of afterthoughts to his seminal late paper on "The Use of an Object", to which I shall return, Winnicott writes about two kinds of being-in-the-world encapsulated in two of Rilke's characteristic notions:

> it seems likely that Rilke, by using *Raum* and *Welt*, gives this same idea in environmental terms. *Raum* is an infinite space in which the individual can operate without passing through the risky experience of destruction and survival of the object; *Welt* is by contrast the world in so far as it has, by survival, become objectified by the individual, and to be used. [1969, p. 240]

The play between *Raum* and *Welt*, between "space" and "world", seems both to represent an essential Rilkean tension and to re-articulate compellingly one of Winnicott's own themes: the difference between object-relating and object-use, between, on the one hand, the would-be omnipotence of the human individual, sustained by an insistent power of illusion, by the unstoppable sequence of his or her projections and identifications, and, on the other, the late-coming recognition by that individual that a real world exists beyond him or her, objectively there, shareable, the object of common knowledge, and unsubduable to his or her wishful fantasies. This is the difference between a world that is deliciously compliant and another world that has hard edges, obstacles, and impossibilities inside it.

The poem I have chosen to look at briefly is one in which these two worlds and these two styles or intensities of feeling are grandly counterposed, and in which the performative energies of the poetic text itself are called upon to create Winnicott's third space of paradox and potentiality. It is the poem without title, dating from the eve of the First World War, which is sometimes known as "the *Weltinnenraum* poem" after the splendid coinage to be found in Rilke's fourth quatrain:

Es winkt zu Fühlung fast aus allen Dingen,
aus jeder Wendung weht es her: Gedenk!
Ein Tag, an dem wir fremd vorübergingen,
Entschließt im künftigen sich zum Geschenk.

Wer rechnet unseren Ertrag? Wer trennt
uns von den alten, den vergangnen Jahren?
Was haben wir seit Anbeginn erfahren,
als daß sich eins im anderen erkennt?

Als daß an uns Gleichgültiges erwarmt?
O Haus, O Wiesenhang, O Abendlicht,
auf einmal bringst du's beinah zum Gesicht
und stehst an uns, umarmend und umarmt.

Durch alle Wesen reicht der eine Raum:
Weltinnenraum. Die Vögel fliegen still
durch uns hindurch. O, der ich wachsen will,
ich seh hinaus, und in mir wächst der Baum.

Ich sorge mich, und in mir steht das Haus.
Ich hüte mich, und in mir ist die Hut.
Geliebter, der ich wurde: an mir ruht
der schönen Schöpfung Bild und weint sich aus.

[1966, p. 81]

EVERYTHING beckons to us to perceive it,
murmurs at every turn "Remember me!"
A day we passed, too busy to receive it,
will yet unlock us all its treasury.

Who shall compute our harvest? Who shall bar
us from the former years, the long-departed?
What have we learnt from living since we started,
except to find in others what we are?

Except to re-enkindle commonplace?
O house, O sloping field, O setting sun!
Your features form into a face, you run,
you cling to us, returning our embrace!

One space spreads through all creatures equally—
inner-world-space. Birds quietly flying go
flying through us. Oh, I that want to grow,
the tree I look outside at grows in me!

It stands in me, that house I look for still,
in me that shelter I have not possessed.
I, the now well-beloved: on my breast
this fair world's image clings and weeps her fill.

[1960]

If we look at the concept *Weltinnenraum* simply in the local context of its quatrain, we seem to be in Winnicott's "infinite space", where the individual can operate without risk, neither unleashing his or her own destructiveness nor feeling threatened by it. "World-inner-space", as Rilke calls it, is produced either by a limitless opening up of individual subjectivity to encompass everything that otherwise lies beyond it, or by a sudden internalization of the outer world, a swallowing of its hard edges and resistant surfaces into the interiority of the mind. Either way, a boundary has been dissolved and an indefinitely permeable membrane has taken its place: birds fly right through us; the tree outside me grows inside me. All in an ecstatic moment of self-surrender, the mind has stopped patrolling its borders, staking its claims upon the world, filtering the data that crowd in upon the human sensorium. It has achieved a perfect porosity that brings no menace with it, no promise of pain; one that offers a supreme reciprocity between the desiring individual and the objects upon which his or her desire plays.

This quatrain has clinching climactic force, however, precisely because the rest of the poem is not written in the same vein. In the earlier stanzas, we are in an animated realm of nostalgia and expectation, crossed by fluctuating affective intensities. The past is available to the human power of memory, but fitfully and effortfully. The external world—the house, the sloping field, the light of the evening sun—strives to meet the individual's wishes, meeting resistance on the way. Even *after* the announcement of the *Weltinnenraum* in which all disparities, asperities, and awkward singularities will be dissolved, a mighty sadness remains. The desired house, the unattained shelter, have been inside the mind from the beginning, but the moment of their being grasped is still not quite here: something continues to resist their unveiling. Something in the world clings to its sorrow even as the work of artistic representation is being praised, and, even as Rilke's own poetic act is reaching its moment of completion, the created order continues to weep. Against the ecstasy of world-inner-space, a disconsolateness seemingly internal to the poetic mind is being reasserted.

Looking at the poem in Winnicottian terms, we could say that it postulates an escape route from the objectivity of the object-world but retreats from the infinite-seeming space to which that escape route leads in order to return to the risky, precarious space of play. Rilke's poetic form, the changing pressures of exclamation and interrogation, the word-play, the comparative and contrastive games that take place between the rhyme words, keep the whole texture of the work mobile and multiform. The intelligence, the senses, and the memory are held together in a mutually complicating way in a playground of in-betweenness. Paradox is rife, accepted not resolved—indeed, it is not merely accepted but made into the major instrument of poetic composition. This is Winnicott's intermediate space realized in words and extending, in a fashion to which his writings accustom us, from the earliest infant experiences to the elaborations of culture. This is a poem that takes us back to our primitive selves—recreating the sharp sensations of childhood, its desire for omnipotence and feelings of danger and abandonment—and at the same time moves us forwards to a debonair grown-upness and sense of aesthetic control. Artistic play for Rilke as for Winnicott animates and interconnects the two dimensions. Primitive psychic creativity is rediscovered in the "higher" activities of the poet at work with words, playing with syllables on the page.

My next literary example comes from Virginia Woolf's last novel, *Between the Acts*, left complete but unrevised at the time of her death in 1941. The central character of the novel, Miss La Trobe, is the author and producer of a village pageant, a modest-seeming affair but one that in due course proves to be hugely ambitious. Her rustic theatricals recapitulate the whole of English history and, beyond that, in her fantasy at least, a much broader panorama of world-historical time. The novel is a comedy of manners, deft and economical, but at the same time it is a profoundly serious, near-tragic reflection on the artistic vocation and the standing of the artist in society. Miss La Trobe is Virginia Woolf's quaint and cranky alter ego. Her wish to enshrine world history, all of it, in her pageant, and to bring that history to an apocalyptic fulfilment on an English summer afternoon and evening, is a parodic recreation of the author's own creative delirium:

> That was a ladder. And that (a cloth roughly painted) was a wall. And that a man with a hod on his back. Mr. Page the reporter, licking his pencil, noted: "With the very limited means at her disposal, Miss La Trobe conveyed to the audience Civilization (the wall) in ruins; rebuilt (witness man with hod) by human effort; witness also woman handing bricks. Any fool could grasp that. Now issued black man in fuzzy wig; coffee-coloured ditto in silver turban; they signify presumably the League of . . ."
>
> A burst of applause greeted this flattering tribute to ourselves. Crude of course. But then she had to keep expenses down. A painted cloth must convey—what *The Times* and *Telegraph* both said in their leaders that very morning.
>
> The tune hummed:
>
> The King is in his counting house,
> Counting out his money,
> The Queen is in her parlour
> Eating . . .
>
> Suddenly the tune stopped. The tune changed. A waltz, was it? Something half known, half not. The swallows danced it. Round and round, in and out they skimmed. Real swallows. Retreating and advancing. And the trees, O the trees, how gravely and sedately like senators in council, or the spaced pillars of some cathedral church. . . . Yes, they barred the music, and massed and hoarded; and prevented what was fluid

> from overflowing. The swallows—or martins were they?— The temple-haunting martins who come, have always come. . . . Yes, perched on the wall, they seemed to foretell what after all *The Times* was saying yesterday. Homes will be built. Each flat with its refrigerator, in the crannied wall. Each of us a free man; plates washed by machinery; not an aeroplane to vex us; all liberated; made whole . . . [1941, pp. 163–164]*

This passage gives the tone, and the daring, of the novel as a whole, but I want to pay attention to those swallows, whose darting, dancing movements are a leitmotif throughout the later stages of the work. These birds are reminiscent of Rilke's, of course, which fly right through us, in one side and out the other. They are "real swallows", the narrative insists, not just images or phantasms. Yet they are real birds that get caught up in the unreality of the pageant: they fly through the scene, extend it into the wider world of the garden, of the countryside that stretches beyond and of the empty sky above. And for a moment or two they dance to the all-too-human tune that accompanies the performance: four and twenty blackbirds are baked in a pie, and swallows fly in time to the birdy doggerel as it unfolds.

The birds are real, yet belong to art. They transcend the wishes of the artist—they will never be a controllable element in the production, for their flight takes them far away from actors and audience—yet they become for a moment creatures of art. They are objects that refuse to be used, yet can still be used. They are figures of paradox. Their flight paths are a play superimposed upon a play, now merging with human contrivance, now winging their way clear of it. When these birds return later in the novel, as the pageant moves to its close, and to its aftermath, they come to mark not just a temporal dimension, but a properly historical one. Each new appearance echoes and inflects its predecessors: the history of the birds in flight is the history of human time as it passes, gathering weight and freight. Woolf's swallows—or are they martins?—take us into the space and time of play, across which dark shadows are cast by the object world and by the terrifying objective fact of human dying. Even Woolf's unmarked allusions to earlier literary

---

*I am indebted to F. Kermode's notes to the 1992 edition for help in tracking down Woolf's allusions.

works have their part to play in creating this sense of knife-edge crisis. The "temple-haunting martins" take us back to Banquo's great speech before Macbeth's castle in the first act of Shakespeare's play, and to the precariousness of the martin's "pendant bed and procreant cradle"; the "crannied wall" similarly enlists a brief lyric by Tennyson in which a plucked flower is held "root and all" in the poet's hand.

These texts by Rilke and Woolf give us, then, scenes that oscillate between different degrees of reality, and of fantastication. The creative intelligence of the narrator is in each case at work upon materials that are both compliant and resistant, that can be moulded and remoulded by the individual's desire-driven fantasies and yet still stand apart from the individual, inviting him or her to let them go, let them be. In both works, speculative activity, and the lively sense of variety, modulation, and metamorphosis that the artistic project triggers, take place under duress. Birds that fly through us, or that fly through the amateur theatricals of artistic endeavour, can leave us lost and wrecked, damaged in some inner core of ourselves. Nothing is easy: the world that delights and caresses us at one moment can terrorize us at the next.

My third passage is from Proust's *In Search of Lost Time* and has about it a similar air of extremity, of playing against the grain and against the odds. It is taken from the section of the novel called *La Prisonnière* [The Captive], and concerns the relationship between the narrator and Albertine:

> Such was my answer; amid the sensual expressions, others will be recognised that were peculiar to my grandmother and my mother. For, little by little, I was beginning to resemble all my relations: my father who—in a very different fashion from myself, no doubt, for if things repeat themselves, it is with great variations—took so keen an interest in the weather; and not my father only, but, more and more, my aunt Léonie. Otherwise Albertine could not but have been a reason for my going out, so as not to leave her on her own, beyond my control. Although every day I found an excuse in some particular indisposition, what made me so often remain in bed was a person—not Albertine, not a person I loved but a person with more power over me than any beloved—who had transmigrated into me, a person despotic to the point of silencing at

> times my jealous suspicions or at least of preventing me from going to verify whether they had any foundation, and that person was my aunt Léonie—my aunt Léonie, who was entirely steeped in piety and with whom I could have sworn that I had not a single point in common, I who was so passionately fond of pleasure, apparently worlds apart from that maniac who had never known any pleasure in her life and lay telling her beads all day long, I who suffered from my inability to actualise a literary career whereas she had been the one person in the family who could never understand that reading was anything other than a means of whiling away the time, of "amusing oneself", which made it, even at Eastertide, permissible on Sundays, when every serious occupation is forbidden in order that the whole day may be hallowed by prayer. And as if it were not enough that I should bear an exaggerated resemblance to my father, to the extent of not being satisfied like him with consulting the barometer, but becoming an animated barometer myself, as if it were not enough that I should allow myself to be ordered by my aunt Léonie to stay at home and watch the weather, from my bedroom window or even from my bed, here I was talking now to Albertine, at one moment as the child that I had been at Combray used to talk to my mother, at another as my grandmother used to talk to me. When we have passed a certain age, the soul of the child that we were and the souls of the dead from whom we sprang come and shower upon us their riches and their spells, asking to be allowed to contribute to the new emotions which we feel and in which, erasing their former image, we recast them in an original creation. Thus my whole past from my earliest years, and, beyond these, the past of my parents and relations, blended with my impure love for Albertine the tender charm of an affection at once filial and maternal. We have to give hospitality, at a certain stage in our lives, to all our relatives who have journeyed so far and gathered round us. [1923, pp. 81–82]

Could it be, Proust's narrator seems to be asking, that when the criss-crossing pattern of identifications and projections that exists in the space between lovers is peeled away, there is nothing there, no core to either partner, just the after-echo of a selfhood that never really was? This passage is one of many in the novel that have a straightforward Freudian dimension to them and that can readily be discussed in classical psychoanalytic terms. The narrator is about to describe Albertine's nakedness, offered for the first time to his gaze, and about to offer a hymn to the sexual conjoining of human bodies. But before reaching this scene of pleasure, he pauses in this passage to ask himself what manner of person it is who has these aroused desires, this urgent drive towards physical self-expression. He finds that he resembles in certain respects his father, in others his mother and grandmother, in still others his hypochondriacal Aunt Léonie, who would shut herself away indoors and think of a strange dog passing her window as a rich and memorable event. The narrator has become again his childhood identifications, and all at once, in a moment of embarrassing remembrance, he has lost all sense of his own singularity and become instead a living crossroads at which other people's identities meet and merge. Face to face with Albertine, he is both a child waiting to be doted upon and a parent waiting to dote. The passage seems to be sketching a portrait of an endlessly dismantlable selfhood: wherever I go, wherever my desire takes me, I am reincarnating and reactivating the prototypical forms of myself, which were in any case not mine and not me. My earliest identifications, as I set out upon the grown-up adventure of sex, are all still in force. I am an infant still, for all the cunning calculation with which I pursue my erotic goals.

One might want to say in response to writing of this kind that the retrospective tenor of Proust's paragraph simply confirms a standard Freudian way of looking at things: knowing about the past is a way of making the present intelligible; a relationship in which the dialogue between partners allows their past selves to continue to speak, and regression to become part of their amatory experience together, is a relationship of a potentially robust and mutually fulfilling kind; the traumatic residues left over from childhood can perhaps by this route be defused, or caught up in another forwards-flung pattern of desire and intention.

What is missing from an account of this kind? What would still be missing if we went further and thought of the narrator of the novel as a version of the analyst figure, listening to the many voices that the narrative contains, evenly suspending his attention across their interplay, placing constructions and interpretations on the speech of others, and on his own anxious and excitable disquisitions? The answer is perhaps this: that Proust's wit, his encompassing comic intelligence, his sense of the absurd, his irony, and his intellectual gaiety would all be missing, or present only in a muted and incidental fashion. The writing we have here, and in other passages resembling it, inhabits a space of multiple meanings, of sustained ambiguities, of facetious implications—a space of potentiality, in short, that can easily be lost if we allow the Freudian contour-map to become too rigid. Part of the wit here springs from the movement of literary meaning across vast internal spaces within the novel and is available as an expressive resource only to the authors of very long works. The references to Aunt Léonie and to the narrator's father's barometer-tapping take us back to the social comedy of "Combray" at the start of the book, 1,500 pages and more ago. The transmigration of souls to which the narrator refers is also a migration of images in space and time: in becoming his aunt he becomes a complete valetudinarian; in finding himself transformed into his father, he finds himself transformed into his father's barometer too. It is because of these people, preying upon him from the past, taking up residence in his present frame, that he chooses to languish indoors, while his lover goes out into the city and thereby prompts in him all manner of anxious fantasies. He could have gone with her, to keep her under surveillance, but he chose instead to luxuriate in his jealous misery. Even when his attention turns to love-making, his ghosts still haunt him, his infant identifications still dictate the variable shapes that his sexual desire adopts.

There is a comedy of the grotesque in writing like this. A large disproportion is installed in the text between the behaviour to be explained, which is a simple, self-defeating affair, and the explanatory procedures that the narrator mobilizes in his quest for understanding. These procedures are vastly expansive in space and time, built into grand syntactic edifices, and overseen by the narrator's boundless powers of self-irony. This is the space between lovers opened up into an arena, a speculative laboratory that, in principle at least, has no outer boundary. The tissue of identifications into which the narrator dissolves his earlier self deprives him of a centralized sense of selfhood, but supplies him instead with an outrageous sense of multiformity and ubiquity. This is textual play in which a childlike sense of omnipotence and an equally childlike sense of vulnerability are set against each other, derived from each other, dissolved into each other, with relentless ingenuity. Winnicott's theory is able to articulate the combined sense of potentiality and impossibility, of inventiveness and restriction, of intellectual proficiency and emotional danger. Winnicott's way of looking at things can tell us a great deal about the internal rhythms of a text like this, about the *Zwischenraum* that it inhabits, about its cult of transformation. Other styles of psychoanalytic explanation, impatient with "the world between", are likely to give much flatter and less stimulating results.

The troublesome power of paradox that begins to spring into prominence when one looks at Proust's novel through a Winnicott lens leads me back to his own writings, and to one of the most extraordinary of them, which I mentioned above—"The Use of an Object" read at a meeting of the New York Psychoanalytic Society in 1968. The following extract will serve as a reminder of the intensity of expression that Winnicott can achieve without recourse to elaborate technical diction, and of his dogged pursuit of paradox as a theoretical tool. There are no showy stylistic feats here, only a very ordinary deployment of metaphor, no memorable maxims, no grace-notes or pirouettes, yet the whole thing is dense, daring, and memorable. He rotates a central conundrum, revealing new facets of it sentence by sentence:

> The subject says to the object: "I destroyed you", and the object is there to receive the communication. From now on the subject says: "Hullo object!" "I destroyed you." "I love you." "You have value for me because of your survival of my destruction of you." "While I am loving you I am all the time destroying you in (unconscious) *fantasy*". Here fantasy begins for the individual. The subject can now *use* the object that has survived. It is important to note that it is not only that the subject destroys the object because the object is placed outside the area of omnipotent control. It is equally significant to state this the other way round and to say that it is the destruction of the object that places the object outside the area of the subject's omnipotent control. In these ways the object develops its own autonomy and life, and (if its survives) contributes-in to the subject, according to its own properties.
>
> In other words, because of the survival of the object, the subject may now have started to live a life in the world of

> objects, and so the subject stands to gain immeasurably; but the price has to be paid in acceptance of the ongoing destruction in unconscious fantasy relative to object-relating. [1968b, pp. 222–223]

This paradox of a destructiveness that creates objects, restores meaning, frees the subject to use external objects rather than submit to their ghostly subjectivity-saturated alternative forms seems to me to establish a bridge between Winnicott's account of the analytic encounter and a very wide range of art works.

I have, of course, been cheating a little in speaking about Rilke, Woolf, and Proust, whose lives overlapped with Winnicott's early adulthood, and who breathed the same air of Europe at war or on the verge of war. For all of them, destructiveness was so visible on the external stage that the artist could not avoid making it his or her own internally. Being exposed naked to the paradoxes of love and hate was a condition of the times in which these writers and their pioneering psychoanalytic contemporary lived. Winnicott's distinction between object-relating and object-use, however, takes us outwards to other times and places, to other media than the written word, and to the common territories that exist between artists at work on the materials of their trade and readers, hearers, and spectators at work on the art work, realizing in themselves all over again the play of mind from which that work sprang. There is no reason at all why Winnicottian lessons about art should be lessons about literature only, or about the Europe of his artistic contemporaries only. The tension between *disegno* and *colore* in the paintings of Titian, or between chromaticism and diatonic harmony in the string quintets of Mozart, is as readily available for discussion in its in-betweenness as any more recent artistic event.

In all these cases the object is being used, destructiveness as well as creativity is being deployed, and ingenious play is being sustained. Winnicott's bare but highly inflected theoretical language is compatible with the craft languages appropriate to each discipline or art or technique. It is compatible, for example, with the language of draughtsmanship, narrative theory, rhetoric, Viennese sonata form, versification, *pointillisme* in the manner of Seurat, or paint-dripping in the manner of Jackson Pollock. With his emphasis on potentiality, and on destructiveness and creativity in perpetual dialogue, Winnicott is in a sense telling artists, and enthusiasts for art, what they already know. But alone among the great psychoanalysts, he does seem to understand the working conditions of excitement, uncertainty, and fear in which artists labour and into which their works may precipitate us. One of the nicest paradoxes in this paradox-filled world is that an analyst who had so little to say about art explicitly, who was so modest in the comments he did make, so reluctant to employ rhetorical finery of his own, should open up a whole new world of dialogue in which artists, critics, art-lovers, and analysts can come together to use objects, and to play.

CHAPTER TWO

Winnicott's Hamlet

Adam Phillips

> This unfortunate aphorism about art holding the mirror up to nature is deliberately said by Hamlet in order to convince the bystanders of his absolute insanity in all art-matters.
>
> Oscar Wilde, "The Decay of Lying"

In a famous letter of 1936, Freud wrote to the writer Arnold Zweig refusing Zweig's request that he be Freud's biographer. Freud, as one cannot help but notice, protested rather too much:

> Only today can I settle down to write you a letter, alarmed by the threat that you want to become my biographer, you, who have so much better and important things to do, you who can establish monarchs and who can survey the brutal folly of mankind from a lofty vantage point: no, I am far too fond of you to permit such a thing. Anyone who writes a biography is committed to lies, concealments, hypocrisy, flattery and even to hiding his own lack of understanding, for biographical truth does not exist, and if it did we could not use it.

> Truth is unobtainable, mankind does not deserve it, and in any case is not our Prince Hamlet right when he asks who would escape whipping were he used after his desert? [E. L. Freud, 1970]

The "threat" of a biography seems to put Freud in something akin to a panic. As he justifies his resistance to the whole idea, he gets himself into a quandary about truth. Biographical truth doesn't exist, and if it did it couldn't be used. Truth is anyway unobtainable, and even if it were obtainable, mankind wouldn't deserve it. This has the kind of implausible, distraught logic that Freud himself taught us how to read.

And then there is Hamlet: "and in any case", Freud writes in a final flourish, "is not our Prince Hamlet right when he asks who would escape whipping were he used after his desert?" What is Hamlet doing here; what is Hamlet being used for? In Act 2, scene 2, Polonius introduces the actors to Hamlet, who gets them to recite something he has heard before in preparation for "The Murder of Gonzago". Impressed by the recitation, Hamlet says to Polonius:

> *Hamlet*: Oh Good my lord, will you see the players well bestowed? Do you hear, let them be well used, for they are the abstracts and brief chronicles of the time. After your death you were better have a bad epitaph than their ill report while you live.
>
> *Polonius*: My lord, I will use them according to their desert.
>
> *Hamlet*: Gods bodykins, man, much better. Use every man after his desert, and who should scape whipping?
>
> [2.2.520]*

Freud's allusion to this scene in his letter clearly has its own oblique accuracy. The letter shares a nexus of preoccupations with the scene in the play. If Freud, like everyone else, gets the biography he deserves, he won't come out of it very well. If Polonius treats the actors according to their deserts, they will, in Hamlet's view, be treated punitively, with insufficient regard. Actors, Hamlet believes, are the most truthful historians: they are the abstracts

---

*All *Hamlet* act, scene, and line references are to the 1982 Arden edition, edited by Howard Jenkins.

and brief chronicles of the time. As though they were biographers, Hamlet warns Polonius of the risk of not valuing them: "After your death you were better have a bad epitaph than their ill report while you live." In the scene, as in the letter, there is something about who deserves what; something about what it might be to provide an accurate account; something about truthfulness. The actor, like the biographer, has to imagine what it is like to be someone else. Like psychoanalysis—one version of the biographical truth that Freud is so interestingly sceptical about—acting and biography raise a question about what it is to know someone. Hamlet will use the actors in the play to expose an unpleasant truth; as it were, to recover some biographical information; to get at the truth about his mother, his father, and his stepfather; and so, of course, about himself.

In his 1964 paper, "The Concept of the False Self", delivered at a symposium entitled *Crime: A Challenge*, Winnicott gave Polonius a walk-on part.

> I think you will agree that there is nothing new about the central idea. Poets, philosophers and seers have always concerned themselves with the idea of a true self, and the betrayal of the self has been a typical example of the unacceptable. Shakespeare, perhaps to avoid being smug, gathered together a bundle of truths and handed them out to us by the mouth of a crashing bore called Polonius. In this way we can take the advice:
>
> "This above all: to thine own self be true,
> And it must follow as the night the day,
> Thou canst not then be false to any man."
>
> You could quote to me from almost any poet of standing and show that this is a pet theme of people who feel intensely. [1986, p. 66]

Once again, *Hamlet* is being used to tell us the truth about truth, in this case the almost tautological truth of the existence and importance of the true self. There is, as it were, a true account in you of who you really are, something in you that you can be true to. There is something there, in Winnicott's case, to betray, and in Freud's case, to misrepresent. You, or someone else, can be your own worst biographer.

It is, of course, part of the rhetorical function of quoting like this to assume that the meaning of the quote is self-evident. Polonius' speech, both in and out of the context of the play, is, as Winnicott intimates, rather more complicated than it seems. "Perhaps to avoid being smug", Winnicott suggests, "Shakespeare put this bundle of truths into the mouth of a crashing bore called Polonius." There is an interestingly implied relationship here between truth and smugness, and, perhaps linked to this, the constitution of an elite group with a shared preoccupation: "You could quote to me from almost any poet of standing", Winnicott asserts, "and show that this is a pet theme of people who feel intensely." It is nowhere suggested in *Hamlet* that Polonius is a poet of standing or, in Winnicott's sense, a person who feels intensely. Crashing bores promoting true selves, or crashing bores being used by Shakespeare, *the* poet, to promote true selves? At its most minimal, one could say, *Hamlet* is about what the rhetoric of truth and falsehood can be used to do. "Your noble son is mad", Polonius tells Gertrude. "Mad call I it, for, to define true madness, / What is't but to be nothing else than mad?" (2.2.92).

Hamlet the character makes a mockery, in a sense, of Polonius's advice to his own son, Laertes, "to thine own self be true". And, by the same token, Hamlet himself predicts what critics of the play will want to do to him, when he says to Guildenstern, "Why look you now, how unworthy a thing you make of me. You would play upon me, you would seem to know my stops, you would pluck out the heart of my mystery" (3.2.346)—as though there were a heart, a centre, to be plucked, a self to be true to. As if it were that simple. A famous, formative book on *Hamlet* by Dover Wilson is called *What Happens in Hamlet* (1951), something that psychoanalysts, including Winnicott, have been notoriously keen to work out—as, indeed, are most of the characters in the play. "What's happening in Hamlet" most of the characters keep wondering, mostly to put a stop to it. "What's happening in my mother?" Hamlet keeps wondering; "what's happening in Claudius?"

Freud, who also didn't want his mystery plucked out by a biographer, or didn't believe it could be—two wishes or fears not always easy to tell apart—wrote in his paper "Psychopathic Characters on the Stage" (1942a [1905–6]), "After all, the conflict in Hamlet is so effectively concealed that it was left to me to unearth it" (p. 310). Biographical truth: the idea of a true self, which, Winnicott says, "Poets, philosophers and seers have always concerned themselves with: the Oedipus complex." And Hamlet as a magnet for the Essences; for all the strong descriptions of the heart of the mystery. And, of course, perhaps the most sacred idea of all: that a person is a mystery, and the mystery has no heart, no centre to it.

As we know, throughout his life Freud was interested in the mystery of who Shakespeare was, keen to work out the pertinent biographical truths. When it came to Shakespeare, Freud seems to have made an exception. Shakespeare, along perhaps with Sophocles and Dostoevsky, was the ultimate, mysterious knower of what Freud thought of as probably universal, trans-historical, non-contingent, deep truths about human nature. But then, of course, if this *were* the case, the question arose of what exactly psychoanalysis had to contribute. ("I have nothing to say," Gore Vidal once remarked, "only something to add.") "The poets and philosophers before me discovered the unconscious", Freud said on the occasion of the celebration of his 70th birthday. "What I discovered was the scientific method by which the unconscious can be studied." All he added, Freud claims, was science: add scientific method to Shakespeare and you get psychoanalysis.

What might Freud have meant? We could imagine, for example, that a group of people called, say, Sophocles, Dostoevsky, and Shakespeare—or Winnicott's "poets, philosophers and seers"—spotted a bird called the Unconscious and produced beautiful, persuasive, dramatic descriptions of it; and then a group of people calling themselves scientists came along—the term "scientific" was first used in English in 1589, about twelve years before *Hamlet* was first performed—and did what? Or, after the scientists had described the bird, what did it look like? What could we do with it, or to it, now, that we could not do before? I am suggesting this not to disparage science, but to show something tiresomely obvious: that psychoanalysis is, among other things, the site for two contested kinds of description that go under the allegorical names of Art and Science. Perhaps more interestingly, if, as Freud said on more than one occasion, "the poets and philosophers before me discovered the unconscious", before science—whatever that is (and clearly it is not one thing, any more than art is)—how did they do it? What did they know, or how did they know what they knew? Unmethodically? Unempirically? Unfalsifiably? Or would it be better to say that they simply used different, historically circumstantial languages, other vocabularies: their own preferred, wholly contingent sentences? From this point of view, to be psychoanalysed or to train to be an analyst would be to learn a language. Or, to put it another way, when psychoanalysts quote Shakespeare within the language of their own discipline, what are they doing? Whether Shakespeare inspires the anxiety or depression of influence—if the works of Shakespeare are some kind of secular Bible—he confronts psychoanalysts, in a sense, with what they have got to add, and with what they know differently.

"I am not so ashamed", Winnicott wrote to Ernest Jones in 1952, "about saying that Shakespeare knew as much as a psychoanalyst as, although I agree that the word 'knew' is wrong, at any rate it is a point of interest for discussion and not a mistake" (Rodman, 1999, p. 33). "Knew" is an important pun here: what is new about psychoanalysis? Or, to move the story forward, what is new about Winnicott compared to Freud? It may all be in Shakespeare, but is it—psychoanalysis—all in Freud? You cannot after all, find words like transference, primary process, dream-work, masochism, repetition compulsion, castration, Oedipus complex anywhere in Shakespeare. There is, at least, a notable change of vocabulary. Saying something sounds Shakespearian is quite different from saying that something sounds Freudian. If I am reading Freud and write a thought in the margin, I am writing psychoanalytic theory; if I am reading Shakespeare and write a thought in the margin, I am unlikely to be writing poetry; and so on. Indeed, that we put Shakespeare and Freud together is itself of interest: that some link suggests itself between psychoanalysis and Shakespeare ties a knot for us. But what is the question they have in common? Why would it have occurred to Winnicott to feel *ashamed* about "saying that Shakespeare knew as much as a psychoanalyst?" (He might conceivably have been ashamed if he had put it the other way round—i.e. that a psychoanalyst knew as much as Shakespeare.) What did he expose that was so inappropriate, so untimely, so humiliating? Was it an affront to Jones that Shakespeare might be more important than Freud, that psychoanalysis was *not that special*, that the question of knowing goes to the heart of something that psychoanalysts are inevitably troubled by? "Although I agree that the word 'knew' is wrong," Winnicott writes, concessionally making no concessions, "at any rate it is a point of interest for discussion and not a mistake" (p. 33).

When Shakespeare turns up in psychoanalysis, it is often *Hamlet;* and when *Hamlet* turns up, the play is usually used to say something about knowing and truth: its difficulty, its impossibility, its uncertain status and definition. One thing that is new about Winnicott is that after Winnicott we can ask: what are psychoanalysts using *Hamlet* for? What are they using the play, and Hamlet as a character, to do? If I were to give this chapter the kind of psychoanalytic title I don't like, I would call it "From Dream-Work to Object-Usage". But to get from Freud to Winnicott—to get from Freud's Hamlet to Winnicott's Hamlet—we have to go via Ernest Jones's book, whose title, *Hamlet and Oedipus*, also leaves too little to be desired. Jones, as he says in his opening paragraph, does not "share the shyness or even aversion displayed by the world at large against too searching an analysis of a thing of beauty, the feeling expressed in Keats's lines on the prismatic study of the rainbow". What Jones refers to, with not enough aversion, as "Keats's" lines on the prismatic study of the rainbow are not Keats's lines exactly, but the poet Haydon's account of Keats's and Lamb's lines in the "immortal dinner" of 1815 to celebrate his painting *Jerusalem*. Wordsworth, Haydon writes,

> was in fine cue and we had a glorious set-to on Homer, Shakespeare, Milton and Virgil. Lamb got exceedingly merry and exquisitely witty ... [and] in a strain of humour beyond description abused me for putting Newton's head into my picture—"a fellow," said he, "who believed nothing unless it was as clear as the three sides of a triangle". And then he and Keats agreed that he had destroyed all the poetry of the rainbow, by reducing it to the prismatic colours. It was impossible to resist him and we all drank "Newton's health and confusion to mathematics". [Bate, 1963, p. 270]

What Jones implicitly pathologizes as Keats's and Lamb's "shyness, or even aversion", Winnicott was to speak up for, but not, paradoxically, by in any sense mocking scientific method. *Hamlet*, as Jones unconsciously intimates, is the rainbow, with, as Haydon writes, "*Jerusalem* towering up behind us as a background."

* * *

> To read Freud and Abraham on the subject of mourning and melancholia alongside *Hamlet* is to be impressed again with the majesty of human achievement. Science and Art here fit exactly; they are completely wedded.
>
> Ella Sharpe, 1929, p. 213

> Freudian literary criticism of Shakespeare is a celestial joke; Shakespearian criticism of Freud will have a hard birth, but it will come since Freud as a writer will survive the death of psychoanalysis.
>
> Harold Bloom, 1994

The figure often rather loosely described by Freud and the early analysts as "the creative artist" seems to be used as a kind of limit factor for the reach of psychoanalysis, someone the analyst can define him/herself against. The artist was a challenge, a provocation to analytic method, but also the occasion for a certain humility and self-doubt. "Before the problem of the creative artist", Freud wrote in "Dostoevsky and Parricide" (1928b, p. 177), "analysis must, alas, lay down its arms." It is a curious image. Does analysis lay down its arms as an act of worship (like not going into church with your machine-gun on) or as an act of acknowledged defeat? The creative artist has won, though what exactly the battle is for is not entirely clear: truth, perhaps; the best description of character, or of what it is to live a life? From a psychoanalytic point of view, it seems, the creative artist both could not be understood, *and* knew things in a way that could not be understood. As though the artist had a secret method, called who he or she happened to be, that was too enigmatic to be known. Or, more simply, unlike a neurosis or a dream, not subject to knowing. Something for which the method of analysis was inapplicable.

But, somewhere, as Freud intimates (and Jones concurs with his point about Keats), there is a war between psychoanalysis and the artists. Can the analyst do to the artist, or his or her work, what Keats and Lamb thought Newton had done to the rainbow, "destroyed all the poetry of the rainbow, by reducing it to the prismatic colours"? Freud's comment is, I think, a wish that reveals a fear: a fear about what the analyst in Freud had done to the creative artist in Freud. This fear, as *Hamlet and Oedipus* makes clear, was not a problem for Jones. "Experience has shown", he writes (1949, p. 11), "that intellectual appreciation in particular of art, is only heightened by understanding." Whenever experience is appealed to—"Experience has shown", Jones writes, when experience shows us nothing we don't make it show—we know something is up. For Jones, art—in this case *Hamlet*—is there, waiting to be understood. Understanding is referred to not as a self-evident good. Jones has some doubt about its value in relationship to art, but no apparent doubt as to its meaning. From Jones's point of view, we all know what understanding is, and psychoanalysis is, for him, a specially powerful modern form of it. There is something that Hamlet, the character, does not understand that Freud and Jones do. Twice, rather obtrusively in his book, Jones uses the unusual Miltonic word "transpicuous", which means "that can be seen through". I read Freud's infamous remark, "Before the problem of the creative artist, analysis must, alas, lay down its arms", as saying: here understanding does not fit; here, faced with a work of art that works for us, we are unavoidably provoked to wonder about what we call understanding and explanation; here we have got the wrong tools, so we lay down our arms and wonder what else to use.

When it comes to art, psychoanalysis runs the risk of falling into the mainstream, promoting "understanding" when understanding itself is the problem. Winnicott, as we shall see, does not stage his Hamlet as someone lacking insight, but as someone caught, in Winnicott's odd language, between being and doing. Perhaps it is enough to say that Winnicott's "hiding" and "being seen" is quite different from being understood and misunderstood. So the question becomes not, "Do we want a scientific or an artistic understanding?" whatever those may be, but, "What do we use this word to do? What does understanding do for Hamlet?"

For Jones, there is "*one* underlying main theme" in *Hamlet*, though he delays as much as Hamlet in telling us what it is; but, unlike Hamlet, this is because, I imagine, we already know what it is. It takes Jones as long to confirm his father, Freud, as it takes Hamlet to avenge his father (Jones's not uninteresting book could have been entitled *Why Freud Was Right*). "The main theme of this story", Jones writes (1949, p. 143), "is a highly elaborated and disguised account of a boy's love for his mother and consequent jealousy of and hatred towards his father." This, of course, explains Hamlet's fabled delay; and, as Jones remarks, the question of Hamlet's so-called "simulation of madness" has also now been cleared up. Before the advent of the new science of psychopathology (psychoanalysis), such discussions were bound to be little better than guesswork and now possess only a historical interest (p. 143). It is the simplest of progress myths: from Shakespeare—from Hamlet—to Freud.

> It is the essential difference between prehistoric and civilized man; the difficulties with which the former had to contend came from without, those with which the latter has to contend really come from within. This inner conflict psychologists know as neurosis, and it is only by study of neurosis that one can learn the fundamental motives and instincts that move men. Here, as in so many other respects, Shakespeare was the first modern. [Jones, 1949, p. 151]

Once again, Shakespeare and Hamlet are being used to tell a truth story: a this-is-the-way-it-really-is story. What is not in doubt in Jones's history of mankind is that there are "fundamental instincts and motives that move men", and that, of course, by definition, these can be learned about. Hamlet, unfortunately, was estranged from his own centre: "Hamlet is stunned by the effect of internal conflict", Jones writes, "into the essential nature of which he never penetrates" (1949, p. 83). The crucial words here are "essential" and "penetrates". In Jones's book, *Hamlet* becomes the site for the bemusing and familiar relationship between the unknowing knower, Hamlet (and Shakespeare), and the knowing knowers, Jones and Jones's version of Freud. *Hamlet and Oedipus* was published as a book in 1949, though some of the work it contains dates from 1923; by now it seems an absurdly naive book. Indeed, it is easy to read it—as I have been doing—in rather the same way as Jones reads *Hamlet*. From the position of the knowing knower, I am as much ahead of the game here as Jones thought he was. Reading Jones reading *Hamlet*, in other words, raises the question—which seems a psychoanalytic one—"What are the alternatives to reading or listening as the knowing knower?" How can we describe this persuasively without wheeling on glib assertions of the wonders of not-knowing or bad readings of Keats's negative capability?

I said earlier that the title I did not want to give this chapter was "From Dream-Work to Object-Usage". One way of describing why Jones's book is poor, why Jones's *Hamlet* is so dull, is that Jones has not dared, in Winnicott's sense, to *use* the play, to make something sufficiently his own with it. It has not been dreamed enough. It is just not *strange* (what the critic Harold Bloom would call a "strong misreading"). Something is clarified, but nothing is perplexed.

So in the language I have been speaking there is the Unknowing knower, whom Freud and Jones call the creative artist; there is the Knowing knower, whom we can call by way of caricature, at least in the context of Jones's book, the psychoanalyst; and then there is the Dreamer, the Unknowing knowing knower. And this brings us, finally, to Winnicott's *Hamlet*, and his extraordinary reading of "To be or not to be" as being about his sense of being and doing, of masculine and feminine elements. A triumph, one might say, of what a cultural cliché—women are, men do—can be used to do. Through crude identification, we can live and speak the clichés about gender in the culture; through dream-work and object-usage, we can make something more idiosyncratic and strange out of what we find.

* * *

> Shakespeare wished to impress upon us the truth that action is the chief end of existence.
>
> Samuel Taylor Coleridge on *Hamlet*

> Immature poets imitate; mature poets steal.
>
> T. S. Eliot, 1951

I want to call unacknowledged borrowing another way of describing dream-work. "Mature poets steal", as Eliot remarked, and, of course, unacknowledged borrowing is a nice way of talking about theft and indebtedness, two issues that were of particular interest to Winnicott. We are, as it were, antisocial in our dreams, able only to steal what belongs to us. In dream-work we steal—from the dream-day, from the past—without ourselves or the world knowing. Dream-work, as Freud describes it, adds a nuance to the phrase "Property is theft". Dream-work is daylight robbery.

Winnicott's reading of *Hamlet* owes an unacknowledged debt to Jones's work. Acknowledged borrowing, we might say in the light of Eliot's remark, is a failure to transform. We can, perhaps, go some way towards understanding Eliot's remark—and, indeed, Winnicott's concept of the antisocial tendency—by noting that Jones acknowledges his debt to Freud insistently and fails to rework significantly Freud's reading of *Hamlet;* Winnicott acknowledges neither Freud nor Jones, and finds for himself a really odd redescription of Hamlet's oedipal dilemma. Hamlet's puzzle—which is Winnicott's puzzle—about the difference between being and doing is not the same as the conflict about incestuous wishes. For Freud and Jones, it is a question about what Hamlet can bear to let himself know: whether he can face the truth of either his own wish to kill his father or the fact of his mother's sexuality. In Winnicott's view, Hamlet does not have a conflict, he has an absence, a dissociation of alternatives. Winnicott's distinction between being and doing is, it should be noted, about truthfulness but not about knowledge. It is not that there is something crucial that Hamlet refuses to know; it is that an alternative way of being is not available to him—the difference, in psychoanalytic language, between repression and dissociation.

Not incidentally, I imagine, Winnicott's other main reference to *Hamlet* is in the talk given in 1950 to psychology and social-work students: "Yes, but how do we know it's true?" In that paper, Winnicott describes two stages that people go through when learning psychology:

> In the first stage, they learn what is being taught about psychology just as they learn the other things. In the second stage they begin to wonder—yes, but is it true, is it real, how do we know? In the second stage the psychological teaching begins to separate out from the other as something that just can't be learnt. It has to be felt as real, or else it is irritating or even maddening. [Winnicott, 1996, p. 13]

The first stage of learning can be called identification: the student becomes like somebody who knows these things. In the second stage, something akin to dream-work and object-usage goes on. Each student, consciously and unconsciously, makes something of his or her own out of it all, finds the bits he or she can use. As in Winnicott's description of object-usage, the students attack the subject with questions and find out what survives. As in Freud's account of dream-work, they find themselves turning the most unlikely bits into something surprising. They make the subject fit in with their unconscious projects. They use it for self-fashioning. It is in describing people using their own real (in his sense) knowledge that Winnicott brings in Hamlet, and once again truthfulness is at issue:

> Perhaps you have been teachers, or you have actually been parents, or you have had charge of people in an office or a factory. Every day you found yourselves surprising yourselves, acting or not acting in a way that exactly fitted the situation, as much as Hamlet's speech "To be or not to be" fits into the exposition of the theme of the play exactly. When you were so placed you could have stood a great deal of digging down into the psychology of your fellow human beings and of yourselves. [Winnicott, 1996, p. 16]

The idea of these professional people surprising themselves, "acting or not acting in a way that exactly fitted the situation", is as integral to something—call it the emotional environment—as "to be or not to be" is to *Hamlet*. The implied image is of a good fit, a non-compliant emotional attunement. "To be or not to be" may fit with Winnicott's sense of the play *Hamlet*, and yet the character Hamlet, in this famous soliloquy in particular, is radically at odds with his world, indeed cannot find a way to act or not act that fits the situation (acting and the nature of action being, of course, two of Hamlet's and Winnicott's insistent preoccupations). Once again, Hamlet is used to say something apparently self-evident that soon becomes enigmatic. It is a curious example for Winnicott to have chosen in this context, given how many well-placed speeches there are in Shakespeare. Whatever else it is about, Hamlet's soliloquy is about whether it is better to be alive or dead, and the reasons he comes up with for staying alive are not cheering.

With uncanny consistency, Hamlet turns up again, in British psychoanalysis, to complicate questions of truth and knowledge. In 1966, Winnicott was to return to Hamlet's soliloquy, to redescribe the Freudian story of bisexuality as having to do with acting or not acting, with doing and being. It is after a discussion entitled "The Male and Female Elements Contrasted" that Winnicott brings on Hamlet.

> The pure female element has nothing to do with drive (or instinct) . . . it leads us to BEING, and this forms the only basis for self-discovery and a sense of existing. . . . [W]hen the girl element in the boy or girl baby . . . finds the breast it is the self that has been found. If the question is asked, what does the girl baby do with the breast?—the answer must be that this girl element is the breast. . . . Object-relating backed by instinct drive belongs to the male element in the personality. . . . The classical statement in regard to finding, using, oral erotism, oral sadism, anal stages etc., arises out of a consideration of the life of a pure male element. [Winnicott, 1966, p. 180]

What are we to make of this? Winnicott *seems* to be trying to describe two attitudes, two ways of relating to an object—and two ways that exist in sequence: first being, then doing. One can *be* the object—Winnicott likens this to primary identification—or one can *do* something to it: one can be absorbed, immersed, or one can use it for some purpose. And the object, of course, can be a person or, indeed, a work of art. To call these female and male elements may be neither here nor there: they do not need to be gendered, perhaps, to be of interest. One question might be: what has Winnicott's language added to Freud's notion of bisexuality? Or is it merely compliant with both the psychoanalytic tradition and gender clichés in the culture to call being and doing female and male elements?

To illustrate his idea, Winnicott brings in Hamlet: "I am reminded of the question: what is the nature of the communication Shakespeare offers in his delineation of Hamlet's personality and character?" (Winnicott, 1966, p. 181). We know by now that when Hamlet comes on things always get more difficult. Hamlet is deemed by Winnicott—and this is rather explicitly articulated in the soliloquy—to have drastically, indeed terminally, separated his male and female elements. When his father was alive, "they lived together in harmony"; but after his death, his female element utterly dissociated from his male element. Hamlet is depicted at this stage as searching for an alternative to the idea "to be". Hamlet's male element, Winnicott says, was "unwelcome", "threatening to take over his whole personality"; he staged the play-within-the-play to bring to life his male element, which was challenged to the full by the tragedy that had become interwoven with it (Winnicott, 1966, p. 182).

Rather than contest Winnicott's alternately baffling and intriguing interpretation, I want to ask what Winnicott's Hamlet is for: what is Winnicott using Hamlet to do for him here? Perhaps Winnicott, like Hamlet, was also searching for an alternative to the idea "to be"; or, in a complementary sense, searching for a description—within the rather awkward context of psychoanalysis—of an alternative to the instinct-driven self. Psychoanalytic theory, one might say, is all about doing. So what else is there? If you don't kill your father or avenge his death, what ways of being, what kind of life is open to you? Do you then need to kill something in yourself, instead? Or, to take this in a slightly different direction, if being is another word for the female element, what is another word for being? (And, similarly, for doing?) In other words, is it possible to say what Winnicott is getting Hamlet to say, given that for Winnicott the whole soliloquy, after the first two words, is "a journey that can lead nowhere?" Winnicott dismisses the whole of the rest of the soliloquy as the rather banal alternative, "or not to be", followed by, as he says, Hamlet's "going over into the sadomasochistic alternative", "leaving aside the theme he started with". The first two words, as a question, are real to Winnicott; after that it is all downhill. Hamlet, unlike Winnicott, cannot formulate an alternative to "to be" because of his dissociation. (For what Winnicott was calling around the same time the False Self, there was the opposite problem: the false self could not think of an alternative to that kind of frantic, spurious doing that Winnicott called, in a memorable phrase, "collecting demands".) One thing, anyway, is relatively clear: Winnicott was using Hamlet to stage what was, for him at least, an abiding opposition. If psychoanalysis had described for us the instinctual self (to use the wrong word), what other self was there? It is perhaps worth adding that we do not see Hamlet doing much pure being in the play.

Winnicott's Hamlet is paralysed neither by old-fashioned doubt nor by new-fashioned oedipal conflict; he is dissociated. He is supposed to illustrate—though I do not quite see how—this dissociation of male and female elements. And one could think that Winnicott is using Hamlet to do something—to pose a problem—that is either, from a psychoanalytic point of view, radically evasive because defensive, or radically subversive. What would it be like, Winnicott implicitly asks us to imagine, to be a person who could not imagine an alternative to being? After all, psychoanalysis is always asking us to imagine a person who cannot imagine an alternative to doing, to instinctual life. What if, say, the oedipal crisis, as described by Freud's and Jones's Hamlet, killed off the possibility of being, made it impossible; if, like a secular Fall, it irredeemably put being and doing at odds with each other, "contaminated" them, to use Winnicott's word? Perhaps, Winnicott is suggesting, the tragedy of the Oedipus complex is that it ineluctably dissociates being from doing. In this sense, one might say, Hamlet does not want to—cannot bear to—think of an alternative to being; the possibility of being has been lost. There is only doing for him now.

But I am as interested here in the accuracy of, the evidence for, Winnicott's reading of Hamlet's soliloquy as in what he can let himself do with, and to, both the play itself and the previous psychoanalytic readings of it by Freud and Jones. The British psychoanalysts' reading of *Hamlet* is a tale of two footnotes. In the opening sentence of his preface to *Hamlet and Oedipus*, Jones writes: "This essay was first written as an exposition of a footnote in *The Interpretation of Dreams*" (Jones, 1949, p. 9). Unacknowledged by Winnicott—and, of course, he may not have read Jones's book—is a footnote in *Hamlet and Oedipus* which reads: "This trait in Hamlet's character has often been the subject of comment—Vining's suggestion that Hamlet really was a woman" (p. 77). This *could* be linked to Winnicott's formulation that Hamlet was searching for an alternative to "to be"; that is, an alternative to his own femaleness. That we cannot be sure whether Winnicott knew of this is, I think, integral to his method, about which, in an infamous statement, he was quite explicit. "I shall not first give an historical survey and show the development of my ideas from the theories of others, because my mind doesn't work that way", he wrote in 1945, introducing his paper, "Primitive Emotional Development". "What happens is that I gather this and that, here and there, settle down to clinical experience, form my own theories, and then, last of all, interest myself to see where I stole what" (Winnicott, 1945, p. 16). This, one could say, is a perfect description of the dream-work. I gather this and that, here and there, during the dream day; settle down to clinical experience, i.e. go to sleep; form my own theories, i.e. have a dream. And then, of course, I interpret it, track its source, interest myself to see where I stole what. The dream-work method.

And then there is the object-usage method. "I recall one Sunday morning calling on [Winnicott]", Masud Khan writes, with Professor Lionel Trilling's *Freud and the Crisis of Our Culture* and urging him to read it. He hid his face in his hands, paused, convulsed himself into visibility, and said, "It is no use, Masud, asking me to read anything! If it bores me I shall fall asleep on the first page, and if it interests me I will start rewriting it by the end of that page" (Khan, 1958, p. xvi). The object-usage method entails destroying something in order to recreate it; as Winnicott does, silently, with Freud's and Jones's readings of Hamlet. He uses them as he needs them, as if to say: without ruthlessness, no transformation; nothing ruined, nothing gained. A lot of the so-called envious attacks described in the psychoanalytic literature are misrecognized attempts at ruthless transformation. It is not surprising that describing them as envious to the patient can be so dismaying.

Winnicott's *Hamlet*: from dream-work to object-usage. Two ways of reading: two ways of relating to an object. Two ways of doing something to oneself and an object. But how can we describe an alternative—in psychoanalytic language—to doing?

Winnicott's soliloquy begins: "To do, or . . . ?"

CHAPTER THREE

"I thought so then": *Othello* and the unthought known

John Fielding

In this brief chapter I try to explore some of the implications, for psychoanalysis and for the reading of literature, of the ways in which the words "know", "think", and "feel" are used in English. The central text is Shakespeare's *Othello*, which seems to me, in an important sense, to be about the thresholds between these words, what it is possible to "know" without being "aware" of. The processes of becoming "aware", of acknowledging what, at some level, is "known", are of course paramount in the practices of psychotherapy and psychoanalysis, and I use references to the work of D. W. Winnicott and Christopher Bollas to elucidate.

My starting point is the heart-breaking moment in the fifth act of *Othello* when Emilia, Iago's wife, recognizes her own complicity in the tragedy: her acknowledgement of the extent to which she has been implicated in her husband's destruction of both Othello and Desdemona. Her collusion was motivated by an attempt to win some demonstration of affection from Iago, by handing over to him the strawberry-embroidered handkerchief—Othello's first gift to his wife—that Iago has so pestered Emilia for and subsequently uses to prove to Othello his wife's infidelity. In the final act, Othello reveals to Emilia that her husband is the source of the—as she knows, false—information. Her response is an immediate recognition of what she should have realized before and an appalled sense of guilt that she did not speak out earlier.

> I thought so then. I'll kill myself for grief
>
> [5.2.199]*

She does not live long enough to explain exactly what it was that she thought or when "then" was, but what Emilia registers is that, at some level of herself, she knew at some point in the past what her husband had been up to. And what she means by "I thought so then" is perhaps less that she "knew" than that she "felt" so then—a kind of apprehension in some senses less certain than knowing, but in other senses more secure. The rest of the play seems to invite us to explore these ambivalences. Othello "knows" his wife to be unfaithful; Emilia "feels" that she is not. Alternatively, Othello "feels" his wife to be unfaithful; Emilia "knows" that she is not. What Iago "thinks", he "knows": what he "feels", he projects onto other people so that they "know" what for him, and in reality, is a fantasy.

Thinking about that, and, in different performances, feeling the intense particularity of Emilia's moment of understanding, led me to what seems a very deep-rooted habit in English, in our present-day speaking, writing, and even thinking itself, of confusion between the uses of "know", "think", and "feel". There is something deeply Cartesian about the ways in which those terms can be deployed to maintain an ideological separation between mind and body in day-to-day discourse—and while that sits uneasily with what is often valorized as English pragmatism, it facilitates a slippage between what are conceived of as different modes of apprehension. Let me try to give illustrations of what I mean. If I say, for example, "I think I am going to be sick", what I mean is that "I feel I am going to be sick". The sensation happening in my mind is probably to do with coping with the social consequences of the sickness, not with feeling the sickness itself. I am warning you that I am going to behave with uncharacteristic impulsiveness and that

*All *Othello* act, scene, and line references are to the 1997 Norton Shakespeare edition.

any sudden rushing from the room does not reveal me as in the grip of something I do not understand.

Conversely, if I say to an opponent at a difficult stage in an argument, "I feel you are using the evidence unscrupulously there", I mean that I think that I see the rules of argument being twisted and that I have grounds for believing that my opponent is being dishonest. My feelings about the argument are likely to be about my opponent and not wanting to antagonize her or him, either by a direct accusation or by any kind of intellectual self-righteousness. I would have used the term "feel" in order to suggest a lower degree of conviction than "know" or even "think" would have conveyed. "I feel" constitutes an appeal to the opponent not to think too badly of me for daring to disagree.

Or, to take a more common-place example: I have a drink with a few colleagues at the end of a hard day. When I eventually arrive home, my partner is fuming. "You *knew* we were going to Jack and Nancy's tonight; I reminded you this morning and you said you would be back well in time. Now we're going to be at least an hour late. I'll have to ring and tell them. Why can you never be on time?" "I *know*, I *know*", I say. "I just forgot what time we'd arranged."

Both these uses of "know" strategically hold off the sense of certain awareness that "know" characteristically contains. The phrase "You *knew* we were going" very deliberately puts the verb in the past tense as if to acknowledge the possibility of forgetting between then and now, but precluding that being offered as adequate excuse. "You didn't think or have a feeling that you had an engagement tonight; you ought to have known—although clearly you didn't." My concession, "I know, I know", hijacks the word for quite other purposes. It means, "I feel the full force of your anger and the justice of your case, and can offer up in mitigation only my feeble sense that although in an intellectual way I know what my failings are, I feel powerless to do anything about them and I implore your indulgence just one more time in not forcing me to face the consequences of my lack of real knowledge of myself!"

One could elaborate many other examples to suggest that this switching of the terms is endemic in the language, and, though one might want to say unconscious, it is purposeful, not merely lazy or confused—if laziness and confusion are ever not purposeful, in their own way. In each example that I gave there seems to be a transposition of the responsibility for thinking or feeling or knowing, which is off-loaded on to one of the other terms. I say "I think" because I do not want to be judged as feeling; I say "I feel" because I do not want to be judged as thinking; I say "I know" because I do not want to be thought to be merely feeling or thinking. I think I am not being fanciful here; the triangulation of those terms—knowing, thinking, and feeling—seems to me crucial to *Othello* and to a great deal of what Shakespeare was preoccupied with in much of the rest of his work. It is a preoccupation peculiarly fitting in a dramatist, who shows rather than tells.

Although in these colloquial examples I am teasing apart the implications of my own words, and the situations are designed to illustrate a point, there are parallels with what might happen in a session of analysis. The speaking, the verbalization, is so positioned—leaving aside for moment the question there of how that comes about—that it has to recognize its own repressions, projections, denials, and unacknowledged motivations and come to terms with what it is really saying. The unconscious becomes conscious, that is. And these interpretations have not been thrust onto the consciousness from outside: they were always there, lurking, if you like, just below the surface. Knowing, thinking, and feeling stop their game of musical chairs and join hands in a collaborative mode of apprehension. I think that this is not quite what Christopher Bollas describes as the "unthought known", which must for him precede the process I have just described, but I am going to use his phrase for my own purposes.

In the epilogue to his book *The Shadow of the Object*, Bollas writes:

> Our psychoanalytical understanding of the transference has always been that this psychological phenomenon is a re-living in the analytic process of earlier states of being and experiencing. But I wonder now if this is strictly true. Can we say that what is occurring in the analysis has in its entirety ever been lived before? I think that in his discovery of psychoanalysis Freud created a situation, now with the person's adult mental faculties present and functioning, in which the individual could live through for the first time elements of psychic life that have not previously been thought.

> Such a view of the transference holds that this is not merely a reliving of a relation to the mother or father, or a representation of the child self, but a fundamentally new experience, in that "something" is given a certain dosage of time, space and attentiveness in which to emerge.
>
> I turn quite naturally to Winnicott's concept of the true self to indicate what I believe this previously unlived something is. However I quarrel with him slightly, in that I do not think this true self should be identified as the id and differentiated from the ego. I think that Winnicott was much closer to the truth when he stated that by the true self he meant the inherited disposition. . . .
>
> At the very core of the concept of the unthought known, therefore, is Winnicott's theory of the true self and Freud's idea of the primary repressed unconscious. . . .
>
> Before the small child is capable of topographically significant mental representations the child already knows the basic essentials of human life, in particular, of his human life. And what is known has not been established via discrete mental representations, in which the human subject forms mental objects in his mind, and abstracts from them theories about existence: that does occur but much later. . . .
>
> We need a term to stand for that which is known but has not yet been thought, if by thought it is understood that we mean that which has been mentally processed accurately. [1987, pp. 277–280]

This notion of knowing as a process that precedes—is more primary than—thought helps me to formulate some ideas about what Shakespeare seems to be concerned with in *Othello*.

There is something about the term that suggests a deliberate side-stepping of cliché, a mode of non-thinking that allows us to rest in what we think we know. "Unthought known" has a wilfulness, a feel of the un-idiomatic, that forces us to think about what is being said, like the translation of a phrase in a foreign language which has no simple equivalent in English and which makes us sharply aware of the differences in structures of feeling and thought between two cultures. Simply reversing the positioning of the words produces, in "unknown thought", a phrase that feels more immediately familiar, something that does have the shape of a cliché, as if it need not be thought about—though what it might mean is not immediately apparent beyond its intra-personal sense: I have a thought that is unknown to you unless I adopt some means to communicate it. It exists as a thought in my head, but it is as yet untransmitted to you. Shakespeare is also very interested in this notion, especially in *Macbeth*, the idea of private knowledge, of thoughts and feelings that are inexpressible except to oneself. But that does not help us to explore the much more difficult, even paradoxical, notion of something that I both know and yet have not thought. It is paradoxical because in ordinary discourse you cannot know something that you have not thought; that would seem simply a matter of logic. But if one looks again at some other perfectly commonplace ways of expressing ourselves, that apparent clarity begins to dissolve. "I knew it", Emilia might have said, or I think we would have in her place. That is our idiom for expression of the same feeling. "I knew it!" What does that mean, or what state of mind does it enact?

One might attempt a number of paraphrases: "My mind had not quite grasped the implications of what at some level of myself I had clearly, I see it now, already taken in"; "I felt what I did not dare acknowledge to myself consciously." Emilia does not say "I knew it", as that was not an available idiom—in that sense at least—in 1606. She says, "I thought so then", which we may understand as "I should have thought so then; I am a fool for not trusting my instincts, for putting aside the misgivings that I could not help feeling". Emilia lived, insofar as she did, a long time before the late-nineteenth-century Samuel Butler, but in her final moments she might have agreed with one of his more engaging formulations: "Hang on to your misgivings, for they are the voice of God." The sense in which I want to use "unthought known" is to refer to, to explore, this area of half-knowledge, one might say, a thought on the verge of consciousness. Philosophically, even psychologically, we do not have a readily available vocabulary for talking about the state—although our ordinary phrasings, as I have tried to show, suggest that the state is by no means unfamiliar.

I believe that there is a very Winnicottian set of resonances here. One set is to do with that characteristic preoccupation of his with what have been called interstitial states, blurred boundaries, transitional areas, the interplay of edges. This is an extremely important and altogether original channel of investigation since it centres on the potential space opened up between mother and baby which is where playing takes place and where the whole of our cultural experience exists. There is much to be said about that, though not here. Another set is to do with Winnicott's thinking about the process of psychoanalysis itself, the area where it takes place and the nature of the insights gained there. His whole approach to the question of interpretation is richly suggestive in terms of the understanding of literary texts. But I want to pick up just two examples from his own writing on different kinds of knowing, one from his clinical practice and the other from a short article he contributed to the *Liberal Magazine* in 1945. The first is from an undated paper included in *Psycho-Analytic Explorations,* "Knowing and Not-Knowing: A Clinical Example":

> The patient, a woman of thirty-five, who has been in analysis for some years, is only just beginning to realize how ill she has been. The nature of her illness was such that she need not know about it, and she has always protested that the analysis started long before she came to analysis, and that it has only helped her to continue a little further than she could have done alone what she has always been able to some extent to do.
>
> In particular she has never acknowledged that she has been unconscious of anything. When the very considerable changes occurred in her as a result of the analysis she always said when she became conscious of material that she was formerly unconscious of "I have always known that," and it is quite certain that she was not just lying as she is by character an extremely reliable person.
>
> An important step in her self-knowledge came as a result of what she had once said to an examiner. She had replied to his question "I know but I have forgotten." In telling me of this, although she was reading from a script having written it down on paper the day before when it occurred to her, she made a mistake and said that her reply was, "I do not know but I have forgotten it." She could not believe that she had made this mistake and hated me for pointing it out to her. And yet it was really the first admission of not knowing. In one sense it was a great advance on what she said to the examiner. To the examiner she in effect said this: "I know this and when I am dispensing medicine I shall be able to use the knowledge,

> and the fact that when I am talking to you I do not remember it is of no consequence." What she said to me was "I know secretly." In other words in the original way of speaking there was a split personality and by means of the split personality she was able to be dishonest and secretive without having to acknowledge it. She knew and she did not know. [n.d., p. 24]

The second passage, reprinted in *Home Is Where We Start From,* is entitled "Thinking and the Unconscious":

> Scientists naturally wish to carry over into their politics something from their own discipline. In human affairs, however, thinking is but a snare and a delusion unless the unconscious is taken into account. I refer to both meanings of the word, "unconscious" meaning deep and not readily available, and also meaning repressed, or actively kept from availability because of the pain that belongs to its acceptance as part of the self. Unconscious feelings sway bodies of people at critical moments, and who is to say that this is bad or good? It is just a fact and one that has to be taken into account all the time by rational politicians if nasty shocks are to be avoided. In fact thinking men and women can only be safely turned loose in the field of planning if they have qualified in this matter of the true understanding of unconscious feelings.
>
> Politicians are used to digging down into the depths intuitively, like artists of all kinds, discovering and bringing to light the wonderful and awful phenomena that belong to human nature. But the intuitive method has its drawbacks, one of the greatest of which is that intuitive people are liable to be hopeless at talking about the things they "know" so easily. I think we would always rather hear the thinkers talking about what they are thinking out than hear the intuitive people talking about what they know. But when it comes to having our lives planned for us, heaven help us if the thinkers take over. Firstly they but seldom believe in the importance of the unconscious at all; and, secondly, even if they do, man's understanding of human nature is not yet so complete as to enable thinking things out entirely to replace feeling. The danger is partly that the thinkers make plans that look marvellous. Each flaw as it appears is dealt with by a still more brilliant piece of thinking out, and in the end the masterpiece of rational construction is overthrown by a little detail like GREED that has been left out of account. . . . I mean Greed, the primitive love-

> impulse, the thing we are all frightened to own up to, but which is basic in our natures, and which we cannot do without, unless we give up our claim to physical and mental health. I would suggest that healthy economics acknowledges the existence and value (as well as the danger) of personal and collective Greed, and tries to harness it. Unsound economics, on the other hand, pretends that Greed is only to be found in certain pathological individuals or gangs of such individuals, and assumes that these individuals can be exterminated or locked up. [1986, pp. 169–170]

Winnicott ends this remarkable little essay: "The unconscious may be an awful nuisance to the thinkers-out, but then so is love to the bishops" (p. 171).

Both of those passages offer insights into the way in which Shakespeare has portrayed levels of knowledge in Iago. Though Iago's first words in the play—indeed, the first words of the play—are a disclaimer of knowledge, "Tush, never tell me", he protests to Roderigo that he knew nothing of Othello's marriage. And he goes on to make many more disclaimers: when Othello orders him to explain how the brawling broke out between Cassio and Montano, Iago declares, "I do not know"; his first ploy with Othello is to reply to a question about Cassio's honesty with "For aught I know"; and he maddens Othello with his first refusal to be specific about what Cassio and Desdemona may have got up to—"I know not what he did". All of these are pieces of manipulation. His consistent tactic with Othello is to imply that though he refuses to acknowledge what he knows, he in fact knows and understands much more comprehensively than anyone else. And Othello, because of doubts about the range and extent of his own knowledge, particularly of women and of what is taken for granted (known but not spoken about) in Venetian society, falls for the tactic absolutely:

> This honest creature doubtless
> Sees and knows more, much more than he unfolds.
>
> [3.3.247]

But, in fact, Iago refuses to allow to himself that he is unaware of anything. His explanations of his own conduct, in soliloquy, are notoriously overdetermined: I hate the Moor because he passed me over for promotion. I hate him because he has married a girl I would like to sleep with myself. I hate him because he has slept with my wife. And in producing that last reason Iago comes out with a revealing formulation:

> And it is thought abroad that twixt my sheets
> He's done my office. I know not if't be true
> But I for mere suspicion in that kind
> Will do as if for surety.
>
> [1.3.369]

Which is to say that knowledge, or lack of it, is irrelevant as a motive for behaviour—what matters is that I feel it to be true. There is a kind of wilfulness in that that overrides the contradiction—he is aware of the contradiction but will not allow it any force. Iago's explanations of all sorts of circumstances are full of contradictions: Cassio got his position because of who he knew, not what he was, and yet Iago boasts to Roderigo that his own candidacy was supported by "three great ones of the city". In his soliloquies Iago relishes his own duplicity, his use of what he can make plausible rather than what he believes to be so, and he presents himself as superior because he alone knows the difference between what is so and what appears to be so—largely, of course, because he himself is creating that difference. But again his formulation of this gives away the extent to which he is a victim of that wilful blurring of the line between appearance and reality. When he, a second time, justifies his antagonism to Othello, he explains himself as:

> Partly led to diet my revenge
> For that I do suspect the lusty Moor
> Hath leapt into my seat, the thought whereof
> Doth, like a poisonous mineral, gnaw my inwards.
>
> [2.3.281]

Notice "the thought whereof". That is, thought in the sense of an apprehension much less solid than knowledge and yet firmer than feeling. Iago knows that Othello's having slept with Emilia is not something he knows—even his "lusty Moor" suggests a kind of arguing himself into accepting what could be the case rather than what is—and yet he conveys how much that supposition pains him. The last line, "like a poisonous mineral, gnaw my inwards", has sometimes been taken as rather clumsy editorializing on Shakespeare's part, in that that is what Iago would feel but it is the playwright's need to let us know that that is what he feels that gets the better of his sense of what the character would be able to put into words. That is a subtle point and is responsive to an awkwardness in the placing of the phrase, but it misses what strikes me as an even more subtle—and true—insight. It is Iago's lived experience of what jealousy is—even when the sources of the jealousy are "known", and the word has to go in inverted commas, to be illusory—that gives him such deep and instinctive sensitivity to the ways in which Othello will react. One of the persistent nineteenth-century questions about Iago was how he could be so clever as to plan all this out, to forecast likely reactions, and to forestall the proliferating occasions for it all to go wrong. The answer is that of course he does not plan it out. Shakespeare is careful to show Iago as an improviser. He has a sense of what he might be working towards, though very vaguely, and what the elements he has at his disposal are, but he has not formulated any specific intentions—much, one might think, like some viciously irresponsible therapist. At least, he has not thought it out until the end of the first act, and even there he sees knavery as merely "engendered". The "monstrous birth"—that is, the bloody or mangled bodies on the bed in the fifth act—he has not imagined with any particularity. All he knows is that it will require a long and difficult labour. That birth metaphor, and it recurs in Iago's imagining of what he is doing with a consistency that shows it to be a deep element in Shakespeare's feel for the situation, alerts him to the potential which can then be left to nature to bring to term. And that allows Iago to both celebrate and minimize his own culpability. The thrill of it all for him is in trusting his instincts and letting himself respond moment by moment.

As soon as he has roused Othello's curiosity (I suppose that is the word, though Shakespeare suggests all sorts of other reasons for Othello's need to know), Iago senses exactly how to play the next card.

> I prithee speak to me as to thy thinkings,
> As thou dost ruminate, and give thy worst of thoughts
> The worst of words.

> Good my lord, pardon me;
> Though I am bound to every act of duty,
> I am not bound to that all slaves are free to:
> Utter my thoughts. Why, say they are vile and false?
> As where's that palace where into foul things
> Sometimes intrude not? Who has a breast so pure,
> But some uncleanly apprehensions
> Keep leets and law-days, and in session sit
> With meditations lawful?
>
> [3.3.136]

Iago knows (who better) about the things we are all frightened to own up to—not just greed but the whole bag of nasty impulses that fester in our imaginations—and, in admitting that, and showing a sense of how those impulses are to be kept in their place, he creates an impression of himself as eminently sane and well-balanced. He both knows and can articulate the dirty secrets that others dare not confront, and in facing them he implies that he has freed himself of their power. Except, of course, that he has not.

He does indeed know things that no one else in the play ever comes close to articulating, and that is his strength: that imaginative, or what one might term potential, knowledge is not denied. Knowledge that is not allowed into effective participation within the self is the source of catastrophe for almost everyone else in the play. They have refused to entertain possibilities. That is exactly what Iago does. And one of the most powerful moments is when he does it through dream.

Othello challenges him to come up with some clear evidence that Desdemona is unfaithful. Iago already has the handkerchief but feels that he must prepare the ground for that to have its full effect. He invents, improvises with stunningly deployed detail, an account of Cassio's dream.

> I lay with Cassio lately,
> And being troubled with a raging tooth
> I could not sleep.
> There are a kind of men so loose of soul
> That in their sleeps will mutter their affairs:
> One of this kind is Cassio.
> In sleep I heard him say: "Sweet Desdemona,
> Let us be wary, let us hide our loves";

> And then, sir, would he gripe and wring my hand,
> Cry, "O sweet creature!" and then kiss me hard,
> As if he plucked up kisses by the roots
> That grew upon my lips; then laid his leg
> Over my thigh, and sighed and kissed, and then
> Cried, "Cursed fate that gave thee to the Moor!"
>
> [3.3.418]

Now there is knowledge there, of a peculiarly lived kind, of the masculine erotics of the play; the dynamic that makes all of these men treat their women as they do, and treat each other as they do, is beautifully encapsulated in a fantasy of a dream. None of that happened, except in Iago's imagination, and yet how persuasive, how felt, it is. Of course Othello swallows it. How knowledgeable Iago is about his own deepest stirrings. And yet can you call that knowledge? If he had known that he knew that, could he have said it—even in that highly metaphorical and potential form?

Of course, when he is asked for an explanation of his conduct at the end of the play, Iago retreats into silence. In his chapter on the uses of the countertransference, Bollas (1987) quotes Susan Sontag on the uses of silence:

> Everyone has experienced how, when punctuated by long silences, words weigh more; they become almost palpable. Or how, when one talks less one begins feeling more fully one's physical presence in a given space. Silence undermines "bad speech", by which I mean dissociated speech. . . . Unmoored from the body, speech deteriorates. It becomes false, inane, ignoble, weightless. Silence can inhibit or counteract this tendency, providing a kind of ballast, monitoring and even correcting language when it becomes inauthentic. [p. 234]

It is a perverse triumph for Iago that when Othello asks him for a reason he speaks as he does:

> Will you, I pray, demand that demi-devil
>   Why he hath thus ensnared my soul and body?
> Demand me nothing; what you know, you know:
>   From this time forth I never will speak word.
>
> [5.2.307]

That refusal, and perhaps also inability, to pass on knowledge allows those left alive to retreat into their conventionalized modes of understanding. These were "unlucky deeds"; Iago a "hellish villain". What do they now know about what has happened? Iago's silence and the silence after the play is ended allows the audience to feel more fully the awful weight of their own insight into what no character other than Emilia has known.

CHAPTER FOUR

On imaginary presence

Michael Podro

The functions of symbolism

One vital feature of Marion Milner's thought was the treatment of symbolism as belonging to human flourishing and not only pathology. This function of symbolism is understood as carrying one's affections and interests from an earlier to a later focus, enabling their transfer to new objects (Milner, 1987b). In this relation, what is symbolized is what is left behind, its interest being transformed into interest of the symbol. And in this transference from the old to the new, the assumption must be that the feelings and interests alter and diversify, just as maintaining the vitality of our thought involves its redirection to new aspects of the world and new potentialities of the thought itself.

> Certainly for the analyst, in certain stages in analysing the artist, the importance of his work of art may be the lost object that the work re-creates; but for the artist as artist, rather than as patient, and for whoever responds to his work, I think that the essential point is the new thing that he has created, the new bit of the external world he has made significant and "real" through endowing it with form. [Milner, 1950, p. 160]

The question that I want to pursue in this chapter is how it is that the artist—here, specifically the painter—can endow things with form. How can paintings—by virtue of their art—achieve this for the painter and the viewer? What is involved in endowing something with form? It is, after all, not a matter of producing some physical shape, nor the simulation of some pre-existent appearance, nor is it a matter of mere fancy; paintings are not mere screens onto which we (painter or viewer) project, as into marks on the canvas or stains and shadows on a wall. For there to be an art—and this must mean an art for the viewer, as well as the painter—the viewer must be able to participate in something that is the outcome of the painter's work, and the painter must do something to make this possible, and he must do this not as an extra bonus but as integral to his own interest.

The spiral of complication: recognition, imagination, and the medium

Let us observe two connected aspects of painting as a starting point. Even the most sophisticated painting would seem to have a very simple basis: that in the marked paper or canvas we recognize a subject—a tree, a man's head, a bowl of fruit, a landscape. But we do not just recognize the look of such things in the surface; rather, we use the surface to *imagine* what we recognize. So there are two factors: our recognition is elicited by the marked surface, and we use the surface—the surface already transfigured by this recognition—to imagine what we recognize.

We might think that simply recognizing the face in the marks of the canvas was already imagining the face; they may appear inextricable because the very notion of picturing combines them. That there are two factors, recognizing and imagining, becomes clearer when we take a non-pictorial example: the girl who traced her departing lover's shadow did not do so merely to make the accidental shadow permanent, but to use the shape she traced to imagine looking at him when he was no longer there. When we notice the look of the mother in her daughter's face, it is not the same as looking at the daughter in order to imagine looking at her mother, in order to represent the mother to ourselves. What is added to recognition is a distinct purpose. While that distinct purpose—imagining—is, in depiction, precipitated by recognition, it also sustains that recognition. But what do we mean by imagining here? What is imagining over and above holding onto the recognition?

The imagining that enters our experience of painting is a way of elaborating on that initial recognition. In pictures, recognition—recognition that triggers imagining—is not sustained in the same way as in ordinary perception. In non-pictorial, ordinary perception, we examine the object we have recognized, narrowing or widening our attention or shifting our position to catch some fresh aspect of it, or altering the questions we ask of it. In the case of depiction, we use the new and peculiar resources that paintings offer us to extend and explore what we have recognized—not what is objectively there, but what we have recognized. These peculiar resources of painting stem from the simple fact that we see the subject in the picture surface and the picture surface as modified by the subject we see in it. By virtue of this two-way relation, the subject and surface can then enter a spiral of complication. To take a core mode of such complication (one found from antiquity to the present and in Eastern and Western art): the impulse of a drawn line may not only mark the shape of the figure but impart to it a sense of movement; movement and shape are projected onto each other so that those quite different aspects of the subject—its shape and its movement—enter a relation that they can have only through drawing. Such complications may mount up, as for instance in certain Leonardo drawings: the striations of the silverpoint do not simply intimate the woman's face or arm, but themselves seem deflected by the forms they model, as if the girl's face or arm were there before the pencil touched the surface. We imagine the drawing procedure interacting with the object, an indication of how we put into metaphorical play the constituent elements of the drawing as subject and medium.

Some painting, like some poetry and drama, makes this transition between the imaginary and the actual more or less thematic. This occurs, for instance, in the case of some Rembrandt self-portraits, because they bring us up against that issue of how the artist as artist and as a person living his life may be related each to the other.

Rembrandt and self-portrayal

When we use the familiar term "self-portrait" with reference to Rembrandt, it involves more than the artist being the subject of his own image.* Self-representation had been current before Rembrandt; for instance, when a painter presented his own image to his colleagues in joining a guild or as a gift to his patron, or when he memorialized himself. In each of these situations, the painter is identifying himself with his skills (Raupp, 1984). But in the case of Rembrandt a distinct genre of painting came into being, giving self-portrayal a very complicated structure, an intellectual and psychological game in which the viewer and painter come into a peculiarly close relation.

There is, first of all, a distinction that we should observe between the self-portrait and the painting or print in which the painter is also his own model. In early Rembrandt etchings, we find him representing himself as shouting or as a snarling beggar (Fig. 1), but on other occasions as the object of intensive physiognomic scrutiny without grimace or role. What these early prints make clear is that Rembrandt himself discovered how drawing and acting can be brought—in his and the viewer's imagination—into a very close relation. This can be traced through the development of the self-portrait in the central sense of the term: the representation of the painter's face—his personal presence—to the viewer. Rembrandt elaborated on this through a series of moves—we might call them conceits or stratagems. While these moves were not exclusive to self-portrayal, when they were coordinated within it they transformed its nature.

First, he invites the viewers of the painting to analogize between their own looking and that of someone in the painting. In the early painting *Artist in the Studio* (c. 1629), now in Boston, we can hardly avoid contrasting the very small panel at which we look and the very large panel on the easel within the picture, and so linking our looking and his. A second conceit is the effect found

---

*A useful volume for surveying Rembrandt's self-portraits is the exhibition catalogue *Rembrandt by Himself* (White & Buvelot, 1999). The comments in this and the next section are developed out of my review of this exhibition (see Podro, 1998, chaps. 3 and 4; 1999).

FIG. 1. *Self-Portrait Open-Mouthed as if Shouting.*
Etching c. 1629. © The British Museum

in, for instance, early portraits of *The Artist as a Young Man* like those in Amsterdam and Munich (c. 1629) in which the head so fills the small panel that the gradients of light catching, say, the cheek or side of the nose lead us to identify the light falling on the picture surface and on the face. The effect of this is that we link the painter observing these gradations on the face with his registering them with the brush. And there are corresponding effects in the early etched heads. This sense of immediacy is enhanced by a third factor: the suggestion of the head's transition between positions and expressions—for instance, in the way the head may be just out of the horizontal and vertical axes, tilted out of the dominant plane (the notional plane parallel to the surface), as in the *Self Portrait with a Gorget* in Florence.

One further factor needs now to be recalled: the painter acting dramatic roles. Such role playing becomes conjoined with the kind of component devices we have been observing, as in the 1639 etched *Self-Portrait Leaning on a Stone Sill* in sixteenth-century costume acting out an imaginary stylish role (Fig. 2) or the 1640 painting in the National Gallery. His presence is like that of the actor on stage, whose movement and personal physiognomy substantiate the protagonist: actor and role—be it that of a famous sixteenth-century artist, a grandee, or St Paul—cannot be separated within our experience. Furthermore, this doubleness remains even when he seems to have cast aside all roles, as when representing himself in the etching of 1648 (Fig. 3) or the late self-portrait of 1669 in the National Gallery.

Painting and biography

These factors taken together might explain why writers for a hundred years at least have seen in the paintings some spiritual or psychological self-revelation, as though, in these paintings, his mind were laid bare to us. Not only are we led to imagine occupying his place in looking at what he looked at, but he dramatically casts off his theatrical roles to appear in front of the curtain as himself. But in what sense does this give us access to his spiritual biography? If we ask how his personal life or self-knowledge could be seen in the painting, we might conceive, broadly, of two different kinds of answer, both unsatisfying.

First, that the images we see are just how the painter summarizes for himself his own life, and so—in seeing what he saw in his own paintings—we have access to his self-understanding. The painting is assumed to have the character of visual introspection. But on any reasonable account, his life is inextricable from the art of painting, inextricable from his painting career, from his discovery of ways of capturing, in paint, the transitions of human atten-

FIG. 2. *Self-Portrait Leaning on a Stone Sill.*
Etching, c. 1639. © The British Museum

tion, or from his endless and intense reworking of Biblical episodes like the story of Bathsheba, or Tobias, or the "Woman Taken in Adultery", or intensifying the complications of self-portrayal. If, in unguarded moments, we have all felt the sense of expressive directness, of apparent access to his own life, this may be because of those analogies between *our* looking and *his*; between his scrutiny

FIG. 3. *Self-Portrait Etching at a Window.*
Etching, drypoint, and burin, 1648. © The British Museum

of himself and the material trace on the canvas scrutinized by us, between his presence to us and to himself, and finally—the last straw—his putting aside of roles to appear as himself. But each of these arises out of the art of painting: "the truest poetry is the most feigning"—and painting feigns by inviting one to take the striations of the brush or etching needle as inhabiting and animating a figure, to take the still surface as the transitory moment, to take Rembrandt as St Paul or the mocking Zeuxis, as the snarling beggar, or as the glamorous young man—and he was none of these things except in painting, or, he was all of these things but only in painting.

Having realized this, we might be led to take up the other extreme position according to which we should make no reference to the inward life of the artist; that we should take these images as fictions, cut off from biographical facts. But fictions, all fictions, absorb and call upon some range of real-world facts, for to be effective they must bring into play our frameworks of belief and patterns of experience, and even specific events and personalities—in this case, the personality and career of Rembrandt. But his personality and career concern us just insofar as they are taken up in the fiction, in that imaginative plasma of the art. To put it in the terms used at the start of this chapter, we are concerned with the biography for how it is symbolized: our interest is in the new symbolizing object that the artist has made, and his making it is itself an integral part of his biography.

Some psychoanalytic reflection

How might these observations bear more widely upon the discourses of psychoanalysis? The capacity of the painter to give something form, to give it significance, depends on painter and viewer being allowed freedom to make connections for themselves: whether the transitions we have traced are imagining the movement of the figure in the sweep of the pen or the complications of the self-portrait. The sense of freedom—as in free association—has a complicated history. Two different senses were operative for Freud, taking up a tradition going back to the late eighteenth century. Both senses implied some escape from rational consistent thought: one was the sense of association, in which different elements collide, fuse, compete with each other for consciousness, as in dream-work and wit; in so doing, they fuse with or partially repress each other, forming structures full of ambiguities and instabilities of sense. The second sense was that of the inadvertent trace, the association that, typically, betrayed a desire or fear. If we simply identified art as the functioning only of the first—the structuring activity, as in dream-work and wit—we would be left without an adequate sense of its motivation. On the other hand, if we failed to include the sense of such structuring, it would not be an account of art. One suggestion of how formal play and urgency might be connected is to be found in *Jokes and Their Relation to the Unconscious* (1905c), where wit is the source of a discrete satisfaction while only contingently connected, instrumentally, with its deeper motivation of illicit aggression. However, contemporaneously, in the *Three Essays on the Origins of Sexuality* (1905d) we have another model of the constructive activity of the mind: the way we recursively restructure the sources of early pleasures into their later forms. If we were to think about an art broadly in these terms, we would be led to ask: what urgencies are carried from the earliest phases of our lives into the new pursuit, of art in a general sense? The beginnings of one of many answers might run like this: one necessary feature of an art is that it is not merely communicative or instrumental, but elicits the participation of the reader or viewer. Taking up suggestions of Winnicott, we might think that the urgency of early experience carried forward into painting is that of uttering and seeking a response, a response that is not merely a copy but a continuation and variation (Stern, 1985; Trevarthen, 1993; Winnicott, 1960, 1965; Wright, 1991). But how does this correspond to our experience of depiction? We might think of the painter's "utterance" as eliciting recognition of the subject or the motif; while allowing the respondent to make his or her own variations, the painter gives the viewer paths of exploration and the opportunity to make connections. The parallel with the infant–mother dialogue would not be the relation of painter and viewer, but that between some initial recognitions or perceptions and the way they become, in our awareness of the painting, developed or enriched or complicated. The theme of self-portraiture might be thought as one of the mythic forms of such dialogue, because, as we pursue its complications, it rehearses the roles of maker and viewer responding to each other.

To summarize: in depiction, recognition triggers imagining and imagining sustains itself though the possibilities of the medium.

The medium is here conceived to include the traditions of pictorial usage and, in the case of the Rembrandt self-portrait, the situation in which painter, image, and viewer can be interrelated through the painting. This historically specific seventeenth-century genre of painting, so I have suggested, engaged with an underlying propensity of the mind, and in doing so altered the understanding and the practice of painting.

CHAPTER FIVE

To make experience sing

Ken Wright

When Freud (1908e [1907], 1910c) addressed the question of artistic creation, he used a method that had yielded rich rewards in the investigation of dreams and neurotic symptoms. The method involved analysing the *content* of a psychic product in order to uncover its unconscious sources. In this way he had shown, for example, that the *manifest content* of a dream was merely a pointer to the unconscious nexus of wishes from which it had arisen, wishes that the dreamer was unable to acknowledge—the dream's *latent content* (Freud, 1900a).

In Freud's view, then, the meaning of a psychic product was discovered by tracing its origin to latent wishes in the unconscious layers of the dreamer's mind. Dream analysis uncovered elements of psychic life about which the dreamer knew nothing, and it came to occupy a special place in Freud's techniques—a "royal road to the unconscious." One consequence of this approach was to place the meaning of a dream outside of the structure of the dream itself. The meaning did not lie in the dream's story line, but elsewhere, in a *hidden* area of thought and feeling that the dreamer could not access directly.

When Freud came to examine literary creations, he employed a similar approach and treated the writer's productions as variants of the dream. Although he was aware of the simplification, he treated the literary product as a kind of day-dream. Putting to one side the conscious elaboration of the literary work, he showed that it, too, could provide access to unconscious complexes (Freud, 1908e [1907]). Indeed, he came to the view that an important part of the writer's skill lay in fashioning his day-dreams (and ultimately his unconscious wishes) into literary forms that were not only acceptable to others, but could also be enjoyed by them.

The ramifications of such an idea were considerable. First, the writer was seen as neurotically impaired—he preferred day-dreams to reality. Second, he used his day-dreams to obtain alternative satisfactions to those that eluded him in ordinary living. Third, the cultural acceptance of his literary productions, and the vicarious pleasure they gave to his readers, provided ratification of his infantile and repressed wishes. Finally, through the recognition that he got from his audience, he could make up, to some extent, for an earlier lack of success in love and social relationships. The view of the artist that emerges from this account is of a pathetic character, indulging himself in a neurotic way. It does not do justice to the dedication and sense of vocation that artists so often possess, nor to the high regard in which Freud held them.

When Freud turned his attention to painting and the plastic arts, he employed the same kind of approach. In his treatment of the Leonardo cartoon, for example (Freud, 1910c), he showed that analysis of certain details of the painting enabled inferences to be drawn about the unconscious fantasy of the artist. Thus, paintings too threw light on what had been repressed in the emotional life of the artist.

This early approach was relatively crude and failed to meet the challenge posed by the work of art. However much it may have given insights into the life and psychopathology of the artist, its achievement in relation to *aesthetics* was limited. While it showed that works of art *could* be made to provide access to the unconscious psychic life of the artist, it failed to illuminate the special nature of the art object. It failed to address why one artefact should be considered a work of art and another not, just as it could not differentiate between significant works of art and those that failed to make it into the cultural arena.

Freud's approach to art was deeply contradictory. For while he wrote of art as nothing more than the culturally approved expression of forbidden wishes, he himself held works of art in high regard and often quoted writers and poets as though they were seers who had special insight into the human condition. In a similar way, his understanding of how people reacted to works of art failed to take account of his own response, reducing it to vicarious satisfaction.

Recent psychoanalytic theory has taken up such contradictions, and I want to mention particularly the work of Hannah Segal, who from a Kleinian perspective has elaborated her understanding of creativity in a collection entitled *Dream, Phantasy, Art* (Segal, 1991). Segal's writing is persuasive. It successfully captures the seriousness of the artistic enterprise and connects with aesthetic concerns in a way that Freud's failed to do. The success of her approach stems from her adoption of a relational focus. Putting on one side a concern with the isolated details of the work of art, and what these might "mean" in an unconscious sense, it emphasizes the relationship of elements to one another within the work as a whole. It is central to Segal's thinking that artistic creation involves work, and working through—a complex synthesis of previously scattered and fragmented elements. What characterizes those objects ranked as art is, for Segal, precisely the creation or re-creation of *whole* objects—the unification of previously separated elements.

This relational view of creativity enables links to be made with the more formal characteristics of works of art that have been the preoccupation of writers on aesthetics. Form, in this aesthetic sense, is a function of how elements in an art object are disposed in relation to one another. It concerns, for example, the shape or contour of a musical sequence, the grouping and relation of masses within a sculpture, the affinity or clash between blocks of colour in a painting. Form is a relational concept, concerned with wholes that are greater than the sum of their parts.

It is hardly surprising that new insights about art came from a mode of psychoanalytic theorizing that emphasized object relations. Although object relations theory is still concerned with drives and impulses, it is more dynamically interactive than earlier theories and always highlights the relational aspects of intrapsychic phenomena. Kleinian theory gives importance to the capacity to relate to whole, rather than part, objects—something closely analogous to the appreciation of form in art where the aesthetic act also involves relating to complex objects rather than a sequential investment with isolated elements.

I shall give just one example of Segal's approach: her understanding of the concept of *significant form* (Segal, 1991, pp. 78–79). An important idea in aesthetics since its introduction by Clive Bell (1914), this concept sought to capture what it was in a work of art that aroused *aesthetic*, as opposed to more associative, emotions. It was not, said Bell, our personal reactions to a work of art that mattered, but particular combinations of shapes and colours that transcended these personal concerns. It was not the specific content of a painting, but a more formal quality that gave rise to the aesthetic response. Bell had been concerned with painting, but a later writer, Roger Fry (1924), suggested that Bell's approach had relevance for the whole range of artistic media.

Significant form is a concept that transcends the particular content of a work of art, and, because it concerns the relations between objects, it may, in principle, be perceived within any arrangement of them. It is not, however, the arrangement *per se* that is important, but what the viewer recognizes in the arrangement as an *inevitable sequence*. The term "inevitable sequence" was Fry's attempt to capture the quality of arrangement that gave rise to aesthetic pleasure. Aesthetic pleasure, he said, was our response to the apprehension of "significant form" and arose from the recognition of "inevitable sequences" in the art object. In terms of experience, the phrase successfully conjures up the "rightness" of an aesthetic arrangement, the sense of the elements within a work of art *having to be* the way they are, as though they match some pre-existing pattern that only now can be realized. To say this is to go beyond Bell and Fry, but I think that such notions are implicit in their language, and they make a bridge to Segal's work on aesthetics.

Segal understands the concept of *significant form* in Kleinian terms, but much of what she writes transcends this relatively narrow framework. In her view, artistic creation is inevitably entangled with the capacity to symbolize. Art is about representation—not necessarily the representation of the external world, but of inner experience. In this view, she is close to Susanne Langer (1942, 1953), who argued that all art is a representation of "the forms of human feeling". For Segal, as for Langer, the rightness of a representation, its inevitability, stems from the sense of concordance between a felt inner structure and an external form that captures exactly the "shape" of that inner structure. It is the "truth" of a representation that arouses the feeling of inevitability. Segal now presses these insights into a Kleinian mould. Building on the idea that a symbol is always constituted on the absence or loss of the object, she argues that the object represented in the creative process is always an object that has been destroyed by the subject's own attacks. The creative act is thus always an activity driven by guilt or concern, an attempt to make reparation to the object by restoring it within the mind and rebuilding it from its scattered and damaged fragments.

Segal's insistence on reparation makes for unnecessary conceptual constraint, and I want to consider an alternative view of creativity. I shall base my argument on Winnicott (1951), who proposed that creativity first develops within the matrix of the mother–infant interaction, at a time before the mother can be experienced as a fully separate object, and thus at a time before destruction and reparation can have any meaning.

Preverbal symbols and primary creativity

The art object is never a straight replication of the actual object but a representation or symbol of it. It is an imaginative re-creation of the object, an object transformed by subjectivity. The matter could be stated thus: first, object; then, passage through subject; finally, a transformed object, which partakes of both object and subject. To give an example: Cézanne talked as though he struggled to create an exact replica of the world, but in fact gave us a unique subjective vision of it. When, for example, I look at his paintings, I clearly recognize the Mont St Victoire, but I see it through the prism of

Cézanne's imagination—it has become Cézanne's mountain, the world according to Cézanne. We recognize the objective landscape, but what we value is its subjective transformation. In this sense, landscape painting is a landscape of the heart as much as a landscape of the world.

Merleau-Ponty (1964) talked of the artist's subjective transformation of the world as the "germination of style" at the surface of his painting. It was, he thought, like the poet's "voice" or the composer's musical idiom. Perhaps it is similar to what Christopher Bollas (1989) has called "the idiom of the self", that highly personal translation, through objects, and within the medium of the world, of the individual's unique spontaneous gesture. Whatever one calls this phenomenon, it involves an amalgam of subjective and objective—a transformation of the objective medium by the subjective gesture of the individual or artist.

Such melding of subjective and objective was a key element in the thought of Donald Winnicott. He regarded it as a feature of early symbols and spoke of it in many different ways—as a moment of *primary creativity*, a realm of *illusion*, and the place of *subjective or transitional objects* (Winnicott, 1951). Winnicott's focus is not on *reparation*—what he called the *stage of concern* (1965)—but on a much earlier phase of the infant's experience in which omnipotence still holds sway. I want to explore this phase through his concept of *primary creativity* (1951).

Winnicott asks us to imagine two different scenarios in each of which the baby is hungry, and in which this state of need arouses a sensory image of the breast in the baby's mind. This image is at least partially based on past experience, a state of affairs often described as the infant hallucinating the breast. Against this background we have scenario one. The sensitive mother knows that her baby is hungry and also, intuitively, how the baby likes things to go. You could say that this mother has imagined her baby's state and now attempts to realize its satisfaction with her actual baby. As a consequence, from the baby's point of view, all the things that the mother provides in the feeding situation (the actual breast) arrive at just the right time and in just the right way—things more or less correspond to the baby's expectation. There is a sense of "rightness" or "fit" for the baby between anticipation and realization, and the feed goes well.

In scenario two, the mother is less in tune with her baby. Perhaps she has less confidence in herself, or finds it difficult to put herself accurately in the baby's place. It is more difficult for her to imagine what she needs to do: her actions are less responsive to actual changes in the baby's state. They are more mechanical, less adapted. So perhaps when the baby gets hold of the nipple, the mother fidgets and the nipple falls out. The baby tries again, but the mother is anxious and tries too hard to help the baby. So instead of things getting better, mother and baby get into a vicious circle of things not working out, not being adapted, not fitting properly together. All the ingredients are there for a feeding problem.

Out of such recognizable scenarios, Winnicott constructs an important piece of theory. In the second scenario, in which the mother is relatively unable to hold her baby accurately in mind, he suggests that the breast presents itself to the baby as an alien object. It is foreign to the baby's experience, and the baby is likely to reject it. Winnicott calls the object that arrives in this way an *impinging object* (it is the baby's experience he always has in mind). By contrast, where mother and baby fit together, the baby has a different kind of experience: what the mother does and gives coincides with what the baby expects or hallucinates. There is a good-enough "fit" between the two. Winnicott suggests that the imagined experience prefigures the one that realizes it and *the baby feels that it has created the breast*. The baby feels empowered by this, and one could imagine the baby feeling, "I have created the world" or, perhaps, "The world is a responsive place (a responsive medium) that I can transform into what I have imagined". (In referring to the mother as the baby's "responsive medium", I anticipate what I shall later say about artistic creation.)

Obviously, the baby does not actually think in this way, but Winnicott suggests that an early experience of omnipotence underpins later creativity. Both the capacity to play, in which we make things be for a while what we want them to be, and the capacity to create, in the narrower artistic sense in which the artist moulds a medium to express his or her imagination—both are made possible by the mother's adaptation. In Winnicott's view, whenever we fashion a world infused with our own subjectivity—whenever, in his terms, we make for ourselves a subjective object—we provide for ourselves what the mother originally provided for us.

Winnicott's focus in this theory is the experience of "fit"—the recognition that something in the environment "fits" and realizes a vital "something" in our own experience. Like Segal's theory, it is relational and object-relational, but the emphasis is different. Segal's creativity is driven by reparative impulses; Winnicott's is concerned with maternal nurturance, the created form (the symbol) fitting and answering the inner need. Segal's creativity reconstructs the destroyed *object* (ultimately the maternal object); Winnicott's helps to maintain the integrity of the *self*. Finally, if Segal's creativity looks after the object, Winnicott's more directly looks after the self.

I want now to consider more closely the creative moment in Winnicott's schema. Winnicott's theories move in a broad sweep, from the first scenario of infant and breast, through the realm of transitional objects and phenomena, to the realm of adult creative living which includes the world of artistic creation in its narrower sense (Winnicott, 1967). I have already noted that Winnicott regarded the adaptive mother as making possible the infant's experience of creating the breast. He also regarded the baby's transitional object (prototypically the bit of blanket) as the baby's first creation after the breast (Winnicott, 1951). What makes the bit of blanket a "creation", rather than mere blanket, is the fact of its transformation. The baby's creative act transmogrifies the bit of blanket so that it is *subjectively transformed*—the bit of blanket now contains an experience with the mother that is still needed but is no longer available on demand. In Winnicott's terms, the baby has re-created the comfort of the mother's breast and body in its new "possession", in order to satisfy a continuing need for it.

What, however, makes possible the transformation of the bit of blanket into provider of the needed experience? In answering this, Winnicott emphasizes the prior conditions provided by the adaptive mother. It was she who allowed her breast to be transformed into the needed breast by providing the pattern of response that fitted the baby's anticipation (we might call this pattern the baby's *inevitable sequence*). But through discovering the inevitable sequence in the bit of blanket (a creative finding that transforms the bit of blanket), the baby is enabled to look after itself in the mother's absence. What Winnicott does not stress is the contribution made by the blanket to the new creation, but the baby can only use the blanket creatively because it *offers*, through some of its actual qualities, the pattern that is needed (its softness, smell, and so on). In other words, the blanket, like the mother at an earlier stage, provides for the infant the sensory semblance of the missing experience.

Suppose that we now think of this new object (the bit of blanket) as a *medium* that allows itself to be used by the baby as a source of needed patterns. We can then discern the beginning of a series: first, the mother offering herself and her body, then the blanket offering its warmth and textures. In this sense, the transitional medium is heir to the mother, who allowed her body to be used and moulded by the baby in the earlier breast scenario. The new medium that the baby has found thus allows itself to be subjectively moulded by the baby.

If we now move on to later creative acts, including the creation of works of art, it is clear that the model I have elaborated from the infant/mother and infant/transitional-object situations continues to have relevance. It suggests that creativity may be based on lack and involves the search for an external form that contains or fits a missing experience. The creative act involves the discovery of the missing experience in another form, and the gap is bridged.

In relation to this process, the chosen medium is important. It is this medium that will furnish a form for the missing experience, a sensory semblance that will partially reinstate it. The medium that provides this semblance occupies the place of the adaptive mother who provided the experience that the infant lacked. I like to think that this creative finding of a needed form carries with it a memory of maternal recognition, and that creativity itself is an endlessly repeated commemoration of this moment.

Maternal mirroring and facial expression

When Winnicott first discussed transitional phenomena in 1951, it was the breast and bit of blanket that occupied his attention. Here, the mother's empathic responses are implicit, both in the way she feeds her baby and in the baby's creation (the bit of blanket) that commemorates this moment. Later in his life, Winnicott's focus changes. What now concerns him is something more visible and less implicit than the mother's bodily adaptation to sensed infant need. The focus is now on mother and baby interacting—the conversation of smiles and gestures, the mother's face reflecting the mood she sees in her baby, and the baby's lively gestures evoking responses from her (Winnicott, 1971a).

I like to think of this changed emphasis as a shift from breast to face—what is now important is the notion of maternal *mirroring*. Winnicott's central metaphor has become the mother's face as the infant's first mirror. It is the way she smiles and interacts with her baby, rather than how she presents her body and breast, that now occupies his attention. Whereas previously the mother's responsiveness lay in the way she gave her body, it is now manifest in her face, whose emotional expressions "reflect back what is there to be seen" (1971a, p. 117). The focus has shifted to preverbal communication, in which the *sensory semblance* of the infant's experience (its visible reflection) is found in the mirror of the mother's face.

Winnicott now thinks of his work in terms of this metaphor—the analyst's words are an attenuated form of the mother's facial mirroring. "I like to think of my work this way [as a giving back of emotional semblances] and to think that if I do (it) well enough the patient will find his or her own self, and will be able to exist and to feel real" (p. 117). He goes on to say that "feeling real is more than existing" (p. 117) and clearly believes that it is the resonating forms that the mother (or therapist) gives back—almost certainly impaired when there is maternal (or therapist) depression—that transform existence into living. "I am seen, therefore I am", says Winnicott, where what is given back is a very special kind of being seen (in the mirror of the mother's feelings) that creates a sense of being alive and real.

Winnicott himself was aware of Lacan's work on the mirror stage (Lacan, 1949), but he realized that his own ideas were different. In Lacan's account, the baby feels joy (*jouissance*) about his reflection in the mirror, because it represents a visual perfection that is beyond his motor grasp. For Winnicott, the baby's enjoyment comes from the aliveness and accuracy of the mother's response, reflected in her facial expression. There, however, the similarity ends. Whereas for Lacan the mirror experience marks the start of an alienation from oneself that is part of the human condition, for Winnicott the experience is foundational, underpinning the sense of self and protecting against the fragmentation to which the self is vulnerable. The image in Lacan's mirror may be intriguing and exciting, but only the mother's mirroring resonance can hold the self and make experience sing.

The song of creation

That the self exists only latently until it is subjectively realized within the responses of another person is a core part of Winnicott's theory of the self. Only when self-experience is reflected does the subject experience himself as alive and real. Winnicott's views on creativity are inextricably linked with this view: only a subject who feels alive in this way can be creative, but, equally, being creative enhances the feeling of being alive. It is thus implicit in Winnicott that adult creativity involves something analogous to early maternal mirroring, as though the creative person, in the very act of creation, performs for her/himself activities that the adaptive mother once provided.

Winnicott's account of these processes pays attention to a limited repertoire of maternal behaviour, and in the following section I draw on the observations of empirical infant research to show that maternal responses to infant feeling states are not restricted to non-verbal facial expressiveness. I want first, however, to illustrate the coming to life of the self in two ways: by quoting from an Aboriginal creation myth and by reference to the work of a poet who was himself deeply concerned with understanding the creative process.

The first draws on Bruce Chatwin's book about the Australian Aborigines (Chatwin, 1987). In the Aboriginal creation story, the Ancestors were old men who lived in a state of suspended animation in the crust of the earth, along with all the other things that were waiting to be created. "All the forms of life lay sleeping . . . dormant seeds in the desert that must wait for a wandering shower" (p. 80). Then the Sun warmed the Ancestors, and they slowly came to life. (Each Ancestor was related in a fundamental way to a particular life-form of the natural world.) As he came to life, each Ancestor "felt his body giving birth to children" (p. 81), the "children" who would later become the forms of the living world. The Snake Man gave birth to snakes, the Witchetty Grub Man to witchetty grubs, the Cockatoo Man to cockatoos, and so on. Each living thing was born in this way and "reached up for the light of day" (p. 81).

All this took place in a twilight zone, with the Ancestors themselves still submerged in the mud. But then the Ancestors cast off the mud that was holding them, and with delight they each saw their children. Each Ancestor called out the name of the creature to which he had given birth, and this calling out—what Chatwin calls "a primordial act of naming" (p. 81)—was in itself a completion of the act of creation. Every living thing that was part of the natural world received a name in this way. The Ancestors named everything, "calling all things into being and weaving their names into verses. The Ancients sang their way all over the world" (p. 81) "[and] wherever their tracks led they left a trail of music. They wrapped the whole world in a web of song" (p. 82).

This story beautifully expresses the idea of singing (naming, reflecting) the world into life. *Something* is there, in a state of dormant pre-existence, there, but not yet alive—latent, potential. Only when it is named and sung—only when reflected in the song of the Ancestors (or in the mother's face)—only then does it spring to life. Winnicott, who saw his own work "as a complex derivative of the face that reflects what is there to be seen" (1971a, p. 117), would have understood this story; so too might the poet Seamus Heaney, who said in a television interview in 1994 at the time of his Nobel Literature Prize: "An echo coming back to you—that's what writing a poem is like!"

Praising the world

Heaney's metaphor offers another way of conveying the importance for the self of being reflected by something "out there". It offers a bridge to the work of another poet, Rainer Maria Rilke, who believed that the poet's task was to "praise the world", even as he struggled to maintain a sense of his own existence. In the

Duino Elegies, a series of poems written over a ten-year period, Rilke expressed his understanding of what life was about and the part that poetic creation held in it.

> Yes, the Springs had need of you. Many a star
> was waiting for you to perceive it. Many a wave
> would rise in the past towards you; or else, perhaps,
> as you went by an open window, a violin
> would be utterly giving itself. All this was commission.
> But were you equal to it?
>
> [Rilke, 1960, p. 225]

For me, the commission that Rilke describes lies in the necessity he feels to sing the world into existence. To reflect it, echo it, and make it live. Like a baby, the world is dumb and has no words. But for the poet, it dances when he sings it . . .

> Are we perhaps *here* just for saying: House,
> Bridge, Fountain, Gate, Jug, Fruit tree, Window,—
> possibly Pillar, Tower? . . . but for *saying*, remember,
> oh, for such saying as never the things themselves
> hoped so intensely to be . . .
>
> [p. 224]

This passage from the Ninth Elegy is evocative and deeply moving. But what is the *saying* or *singing* that Rilke talks about, the saying or singing that brings the world and experience into existence? I think that the poet is telling us that singing, saying, dancing, painting, sculpting—whatever medium the artist chooses to work in—each of these activities in their own way *create* the artist's experience. As for the baby, experience is latent until it finds a form.

> Yes! The springs had need of you.
> Many a star
> was waiting for you to perceive it . . .

Rilke sees the artist responding, out of a kind of love, to what he takes to be the mute need of Earth:

> Earth. Is it not this that you want,
> to arise invisibly in us? . . .

And he goes on:

> These things that live on departure
> understand when you praise them: fleeting, they look for
> rescue through something in us, the most fleeting of all.
> Want us to change them entirely, within our invisible hearts,
> into—oh, endlessly—into ourselves, whosoever we are.
>
> [p. 245]

Rilke, the poet, does not need another of Earth's spring times to win him over—to make him sing its praises, and transform it into a different kind of existence within the new and communicable realm of the artist's feelings. He cries out, as though in ecstasy: "Earth, you Darling, I will" (p. 245).

These passages give powerful expression to the idea that the poet, and perhaps every artist, is engaged in a "love affair with the world" (Greenacre, 1957), which causes him or her to "sing" the world, or to "praise" it, to give back to the world what the world has previously given, or shown to, him or her. The artist sets about this task by finding forms that, as Winnicott says, "reflect what is there to be seen". But this is no passive reflection or saying. It is "such saying as never the things themselves hoped so intensely to be", a passionate saying that creates a sensory semblance, a living form of the thing or experience itself, including the way the world has come alive in the artist's feelings. It is the artist's task to give back to the world this living semblance, and in so doing to give it the life it lacked before. This is the sense in which the poet or artist sings the world into existence, and, as the Aboriginal story puts it, "wraps the whole world in a web of song".

Creating the self

There is a circularity in this creative "singing" or "saying", a dialogue with the world that results in each party (world and self) becoming more alive. As the world is transformed by the creative utterance ("endlessly, oh, endlessly into ourselves . . ."), so the artists themselves are transformed by the world—through their own visionary seeing and praising of it. As Susanne Langer (1953) says in her book *Feeling and Form*, the artist "finds forms for human feeling", but equally, these forms are the forms of the world that the artist has discovered. It is as though the artist said to the world: "I have felt you, world—the rhythm and pulse of your life—and I am singing it, giving it back to you, giving you back the way you live in me!" If Rilke is right, we can begin to understand the way artists find their own life and voice in the very moment when they feel they have given life and voice to the mute world. Even as they praise the world, they give form to their own feeling. What artists create, in their passionate engagement with their medium, is a subjectively transformed object—or, as Winnicott says, a *subjective object*.

It is the ability of artists to sing the song of themselves—simultaneously the song of the world—that lies at the heart of their creativity. In the process of creating a work of art, the artists' medium is actively transformed until it becomes expressive of their subjective experience. In one way or another, it is constrained and worked upon until it *becomes* the required and resonating form for their subjective life. *It is forced by the artists to sing their inner song.* If the mother or Ancestor sang the original song that created self or world, the artists must now sing this song for themselves because their life or liveliness depends upon it.

There is of course, a paradox in what I am saying. On the one hand, artists sing the world into existence; they place themselves at the service of the world because they love the world so much. On the other hand, they ruthlessly force the world, or that part of it which is their chosen medium, to respond to them in the resonating way they want. The medium must now be at their service. Artists—which means all of us at one time or another—will not give up until they have forced or coaxed the paint, the musical score, the piece of stone, the words on the bit of paper or the word-processing screen to sing to them their own song. In Walt Whitman's terms, they must sing the *Song of Myself*.

The mother's song—attunement

I now want to consider another kind of "singing", in which the mother's response can be seen as life enhancing. In moving back and forth between the activity of the artist and the early activity of the mother in relation to her baby, I hope to make clearer links that may exist between these two fields.

In speaking of the mother's responsiveness, I have largely confined myself to Winnicott's formulations: firstly concerning the adaptive mother who gives to the baby the searched for bodily response, secondly concerning the more communicative response mediated by the mother's facial mirroring. However, although both responses are important for the infant, they do not take account of the full variety of behavioural means through which a mother may communicate and "sing" her baby. The findings of empirical infant research suggest other ways, and I draw attention to one particular idea—maternal attunement—which has been beautifully developed by Daniel Stern (1985, pp. 138–161).

Observational studies have shown that mothers not only respond to their infants' major emotions (sometimes called the *categorical affects*); they also respond, in a moment-by-moment way, to the smaller changes of excitement and arousal that accompany everything the baby does (called by Stern the *vitality affects*). The mother tracks these smaller changes as we track a tennis player during an exciting game—she reads her baby by every possible non-verbal means and intuitively senses the changing pattern of its feeling state: the contours of arousal, the rhythms of excitement, its urgent strivings and triumphant satisfactions. She follows the baby with a close yet barely conscious attention that teaches her the changing pattern of its experience. Stern gives the name *attunement* to this tracking process—attunement to the infant's vitality affects.

In the normal situation, the mother does not merely register the infant's state in an ongoing way: she engages in responsive displays of her own, which, in one modality or another, reflect the patterns and rhythms of the baby's vitality affects. If, for example, the baby is reaching for a toy, the mother may make a series of movements or sounds that reflect or resonate to the baby's changing pattern of excitement. It is as though she plays back to the baby what she has just experienced in identification with it. Often the mother's response exaggerates the baby's pattern, making the pattern more apparent; or the response may be cast in another sensory mode than the baby's display, giving it a difference as well as a similarity. It is this combination of similarity *and* difference—the *transformation* of the baby's pattern—which prompts Stern to describe attunement as the "recasting of an affective state" (1985, p. 161). This mini-enactment or portrayal of the baby's state not only gives back to the baby what the baby has just revealed; equally, it gives back to the baby something of the mother's uniquely personal stamp. What comes back is like an echo, albeit an echo creatively changed by its passage through the mother.

The link of such ideas with artistic creativity is inescapable: "An echo coming back to you—that is what writing a poem is like", said Seamus Heaney; an echo of the artist's self, transformed by a passage through the world. And perhaps it is the same with painting a canvas or writing a symphony, or seeing oneself reflected in the face of the person whom one loves. Not least, this is a way of thinking about therapy itself, as Winnicott (1971a) himself so eloquently expressed: "Psychotherapy is not making clever and apt interpretations; by and large it is a long term giving back to the patient what the patient brings. It is a complex derivative of the face that reflects what is there to be seen" (p. 117).

Artistic creativity and attunement

I have discussed attunement because it enlarges our conception of what it means to have something given back in a transformed and enlivening way, because experiences of this kind are evidently vital to the growing self, especially to the sense of feeling alive and real (both Stern and Winnicott would make this claim), and because the need for such experiences may well continue throughout life: we never lose the need for affirmation and reflection. I am claiming that we have to feel ourselves alive within another person to feel alive within ourselves, and that such a need is basic to our social nature—it makes the difference, in Winnicott's terms, between "feeling real" and merely "existing".

Winnicott understood creativity as a way of living life; it was not just the province of artists and poets but potentially within reach of us all. Although he did not put it in quite these terms, he thought of the world, particularly the world of other people, as constituting a kind of medium that a person approaches with a particular attitude. Where there has been a sufficient experience of the environment meeting her or his inner dispositions adaptively, it will be possible for the adult to approach it in a creative way, with the expectation that it can be transformed to some extent by her or his need. Only when the environment has been excessively unkind and impinging will the adult be unable to find within her/himself a creative stance towards it.

In artistic creation, the creative attitude is seen in its clearest form, and Stern's work on attunement extends and enriches Winnicott's understanding of it. From this perspective, the fundamental project of art is the process of discovering, or making, forms that resonate with the artist's deepest self. Such a process is developmentally earlier, and in that sense more basic, than the impulse towards reparation that underpins the Klein/Segal theory of art. The need to find forms for the self is an existential one. What is in question is the basic sense of subjective being, and this must surely precede any question of the self's guilt.

It is my contention that the need to find forms for the self's experience is as basic as the need for satisfaction of bodily needs: the need for the mother's responding face is as great as the need for her breast and milk. I have argued that the discovery of such forms is rooted in the early relationship with the mother—the dialogue with her face and breast—and continues with increasing complexity through the more social, yet still preverbal, experiences of attunement.

Winnicott claimed that the earliest transitional phenomena looked backward towards the breast and the adaptive mother, and forward towards later cultural creations, so that there was continuity between earlier and later phenomena. Stern's work suggests that a wider group of maternal responses might be meaningfully inserted into this developmental path, the mother's attuned enactments providing fertile ground for later cultural forms. The baby's transitional object gives to the baby a degree of independence from the actual mother, enabling the baby to create for itself a sense of her presence and responsiveness. In similar fashion, artistic creation may fulfil a comparable function for the artist (and, of course, for the audience, though that is another discussion); it enables him or her to look after him/herself through the recognition and resonance of the forms he or she is able to make.

Creativity and maternal deficit

If artists are those who dedicate their life, in an almost compulsive way, to the creation of emotionally resonating forms, what is it that leads them to do this? Is it, as Freud said, that they hope thereby to achieve the love and recognition they have failed to achieve by ordinary means? Or is it, as Segal suggests, that their destructiveness towards their objects is so great that they have to work ceaselessly to repair them?

By placing the impetus for creativity firmly within the preverbal layers of the mind, it is clear that I do not regard either of these as the case. Is it, then, that the artists' work is a celebration of the mother of infancy, who attended so closely to their emotional needs? Or is it somehow the reverse of this: that artists are those who know what they want—they have had a taste of attuning experience, but not enough—and now feel that their lives depends on creating it for themselves? Are they, in short, those who have had a relatively depriving experience in the area of attunement—a crisis of confidence in the mother, perhaps—which has made them feel that the only security would lie in creating the forms they needed for themselves?

Perhaps the example of Rilke, whose evocations of the poet's task I have already quoted, may clarify these alternatives. Rilke is a lyrical, and sometimes ecstatic poet, whose love of the world, and his need to praise it, knew no bounds. If ever a poet *sang* the world, it was surely Rilke. Yet Rilke had an appallingly unhappy and lonely childhood. His mother was narcissistic and thoroughly self-involved. She had desperately wanted a girl, and for the first few years of Rilke's life had virtually brought him up as one. She had curled his hair, dressed him in little girls' clothes, and no doubt discouraged any expression of his masculinity. Even his name, Maria, was a girl's name (Britton, 1998). In Winnicott's terms, she was highly *impinging*, in Stern's terms, almost totally lacking in attunement. She must have been impervious to her son's experience, caring only about the fulfilment of her own fantasies through him. The young Rilke must have felt constant doubt about his own reality, and there must have been a serious deficit of containing forms in his mother's responses to him.

Given such disconfirming experience, some children might have given up and died emotionally. But Rilke kept himself alive and discovered in himself a means of creating and finding the forms that he needed. His poetic vocation can be seen as his recognition that this was the most important thing he had to do: to create and re-create the responsive mother he had lacked. When, as in the *Duino Elegies*, he sees his task as a redeeming of the world through his singing or praising it, we can now see him as being the mother that he never had. In similar fashion, we can see the mute Earth that is waiting to be recognized as his own mute self, waiting upon the life-giving response of the poet-mother, who is now also himself.

This brief account of Rilke's childhood supports the idea that the artist's life struggle is to draw his or her object/medium into an expressive and responsive state. From this point of view, it is not so much that the object has been damaged or destroyed by the artist's aggression and needs to be repaired (Klein/Segal), but rather that the artist is struggling with a deficit, brought about through maternal failure and lack of maternal response (Winnicott). In this sense, the artist's creative work on the object is as an attempt to repair or restore the object's capacity to respond—perhaps even to create such a responsive object for the first time: "This is the creature there has never been . . ." writes Rilke, in the *Sonnets to Orpheus*. Rilke's quest—and perhaps the quest of every artist—is for a medium that *will* respond, that *cannot* now escape his or her shaping influence, a medium that can be persuaded or forced to yield the expression that is needed, a medium more under the artist's control than the mother herself was. As Winnicott saw, it is here that the ruthlessness of the artist comes into play, the use of omnipotence to *make* the world be what the self desires. In the course of realizing this project, the self is restored, though the task is never completed once and for all. The artist lives always on the edge of a no-mother space, and hence the compulsion to go on creating.

Conclusion

My aim in this paper has been to develop a Winnicottian approach to art that differs significantly both from Freud's early essays in the field, and from the more recent Kleinian approach of Hannah Segal. Freud's theoretical equipment was too deeply rooted in instinct theory to do justice to the relational aspects of the work of art, while Segal's view pays too little attention to the power and influence of the actual environment in shaping the course of development, and the subsequent life of the individual.

I have attempted to build on Winnicott's interest in creativity and its roots in the early mother–infant set-up. In particular, I have made use of his notion of *primary creativity* which can only be understood in terms of a very specific kind of interaction with the mother. I have already noted that Winnicott's views evolved significantly, and in his later work he shifts into a more social and communicational framework (Winnicott, 1971a). This shift constitutes a major change in thinking about early development. It is not that the intrapsychic is now ignored, but seen as shaped and engraved by preverbal communicational events.

This new way of thinking allows bridges to be made between Winnicott's work and the field of empirical infant research—it is here that the work of Stern has been important to my own understanding. Stern too is concerned with interactive events between mother and infant, and his concept of attunement fills a gap in Winnicott's thinking. It addresses what happens after the period of transitional activity, when the baby is beginning to separate more completely from the mother, the period of Mahler's *separation-individuation* (Mahler, Pine, & Bergman, 1975). This is a time when keeping in touch with the mother acquires a new dimension, such contact having to be maintained across actual space. Facial mirroring goes some way to bridging this gap but the notion of attunement allows for a more diverse kind of connectedness that covers the whole range of sensory modalities, and is better able to span the increasing physical distance.

It is possible to see attunement as the providing the beginnings of a preverbal "language" between mother and infant which ensures that the infant can still feel at one with the mother during separation. It is a versatile "language" that passes freely from one sensory channel to another, while being highly supportive and containing of infant experience. It seems well adapted, not only to alleviating the sense of separateness, but also to bridging the passage into language proper. In this regard, Stern stresses that attunement is at its height towards the end of the preverbal period.

It is the notion of a preverbal "language" supportive of the self that lends itself to a new way of thinking about artistic creativity. Langer (1942, 1953) argues that artistic creation also makes use of non-verbal "languages" which span a range of sensory modalities and, like attunement, operate with iconic symbols. For Langer, such symbols are not so much symbols in the psychoanalytic sense, of referring to, or embodying, specific unconscious fantasies, as iconic representations that give form to human feeling. This highly suggestive, though general formulation points to the shapes, rhythms and textures of human experience rather than to its context-bound details. It is, of course, to just such shapes and rhythms that attunement also refers.

Whether this new way of thinking will illuminate the artist's choice of medium remains to be seen. I have not addressed the issue in this paper. But if the matching of patterns between mother and infant is indeed important in laying the foundations of a secure self, it is not improbable that the preverbal attunement "language" that develops between a particular mother and baby will affect that baby's later preferences in the area of self-maintenance.

Responsive dialogue involves a matching resonance of form and experience. It underpins the development of the self and the core sense of "aliveness"; it also underpins the work of the creative artist. In this view, the core of creativity resides in the ability to make (or find) forms that fit experience—artists are those who have developed this capacity to an extraordinary degree. I have proposed that artists engage in this activity because they have to—as means of survival in the face of a mother poorly attuned, emotionally absent, or erratic to the point of trauma. Artists may believe that they are singing the *world* into existence, as did Rilke, but even more, they are singing *to themselves* the needed maternal song, and breathing *themselves* from existence into life.

CHAPTER SIX

Creativity, playing, dreaming: overlapping circles in the work of Marion Milner and D. W. Winnicott

Vincenzo Bonaminio & Mariassunta Di Renzo

"Toys are things that want to be played with . . ."

Ilaria, 8 years old

In her 1952 article, "The Role of Illusion in Symbol Formation", Marion Milner offers some considerations on the receptive function of toys and the nature of play as boundary between inside and outside with reference to the analysis of an 11-year-old child, whom she later refers to as "Simon":

> he frequently adopted a particularly bullying tone when talking to me . . ., but he always dropped this tone as soon as he began imaginative play with the toys. This observation suggested that perhaps this boy could drop the hectoring tone, during this kind of play, because it was a situation in which he could have a different kind of relation to external reality, by means of the toys; he could do what he liked with them and yet they were outside him. . . . as soon as he had settled down to using the toys as a pliable medium, external to himself, but not insisting on their own separate objective existence, then apparently he could treat me with friendliness and con-

> sideration, and even accept real frustration from me. . . . In the play with toys there was something half-way between day-dreaming and purposeful instinctive or expedient action. As soon as he moved a toy in response to some wish or fantasy then the play-village was different, and the new sight set off a new set of possibilities; just as in free imaginative drawing, the sight of a mark made on the paper provokes new associations. [p. 92]

In our view, this passage shows a conception of play in the consulting-room as a potentially creative experience for the child, characterized by those factors that, according to Milner, favour artistic experience: (1) muscular action with a medium, a little bit of the outside world that was malleable, such as chalk or paint, (2) within a limited space, a frame, a sheet of paper, a wall, (3) a sacrifice of deliberative action or working to a plan, instead allowing the hand and eye to play with the medium (1952, p. 80). Similarly we could say that, in playing, the *framework*—the space–time of the analytic session—allows the child to use toys subjectively as the malleable material of external reality while activating imagination and fantasy.

"Toys are things that want to be played with . . ." said Ilaria, an 8-year-old child in analysis with one of us, stressing with this paradoxical image that, while toys, without the meanings and intentions of those who use them, are only "things", it is precisely their malleable qualities that allow those meanings to be generated.

The function of playing as a bridge between internal and external can be assimilated to Marion Milner's conception of art, since both play and art can be seen to "link the world of subjective 'unreality' and 'object reality' harmoniously fusing the edges, but not confusing them" (1952a, p. 128). In both play and art, the *illusion of oneness* is crucial, the fusion of *me* and *not me* which expresses faith in a personally created reality. For Milner, the internal need to discover oneness in diversity, as an expression of a basic need for internal consistency, constitutes the fundamental role of illusion in symbol formation. She proposes that "these states of *illusion of oneness* are a necessary phase in the continued growth of the sense of twoness". One cannot reach the phase where disillusionment—that is, the acknowledgement of identity, diversity, and separateness—can be tried out, without first having had time to experience the illusion of oneness and the non-distinction between subject and object.

Playing and art, then, share the same paradox: through the form given to it, play, like art, makes the "not-me" real and understandable by infusing "not-me" objective material with subjective "me" psychic content (Milner, 1957, p. 228). In this sense, the child's creative experience of playing in the consulting-room cannot be induced or shared by the analyst. The analyst's function is to provide the conditions for this subjective experience to be realized, providing a "framed space" analogous to a blank page for drawing or painting.

Milner's reflections on creativity, the illusion of non-separation of object and subject, and the mind's capacity to symbolize evidently share much in common with Winnicott's ideas of transitional phenomena and potential space (1951). Their encounter is generally held to have been formative and productive for both, something confirmed by Milner herself in a paper given to the British Psycho-Analytical Society in 1972, at a memorial meeting for Winnicott. Milner stressed how the experience of shared images had been a transitional process for both of them: a two-way journey that facilitated both a mutual exchange of views and the forging of two personal, subjective idioms. Milner writes:

> And from this picture of the water's surface I come to one of his images, that is, the quotation from Tagore that he put at the head of his paper "The Location of Cultural Experience". "On the sea-shore of endless worlds children play". I too have had this line at the back of my mind, ever since I first read it in 1915. Winnicott said that, for him, the aphorism aided speculation upon the question, if play is neither inside nor outside, where is it? For me it stirred thoughts of the coming and going of the tides, the rhythmic daily submergence and smoothing out of this place where children play.
>
> Later in this paper about the place of cultural experience he uses another image that we both had in common—only I had completely forgotten about it. He is talking about how the baby comes to be able to make use of the symbol of union and can begin to allow for and benefit from separation, a separa-

> tion that is not a separation, but a form of union; and here he refers to a drawing that I made long ago in the 1930s, showing the interplay of the edges of two jugs. He says the drawing conveyed to him the tremendous significance there can be in the interplay of edges.
>
> I too found myself using this same drawing as a visual symbol for his concept of potential space. [1972, pp. 312–313]

This drawing, which for Milner anticipated the image of overlapping circles later invoked by her patient Susan, also expressed how she perceived her own work with patients (Milner, 1977). It provides a useful image of the mutual creative interaction between Milner and Winnicott.

Following their example, we aim to highlight these *emerging aspects of experience* in playing and the dream and relate them to creativity, a topic already discussed in an earlier study (Bonaminio & Di Renzo, 1996). Our starting point is an extract from the analysis of a 5-year-old child, which serves to illustrate the personal sense assumed by play in the borderline between external and internal, on the threshold of subjective and objective.

Playing and experiencing

> At the end of a session in the second year of analysis with 5-year-old "Matilde" the analyst is left with the somewhat depressing feeling that "nothing happened", notwithstanding the wealth of clinical material which showed a clearly manic tendency (which had been interpreted). The child had spent almost the whole time doing gymnastics, asking to go to the bathroom, starting and interrupting games, asking the analyst to recite with her nursery rhymes learnt at school. At the end of the session, the child's mother comes to fetch her and engages the analyst in conversation, evidently eager for some attention herself. The mother tells the analyst, who is exhausted and dissatisfied with the unproductive session, how Matilde, who has worn glasses since she was 2, had been to the optician the previous day. The analyst listens to the mother, whose manner

> is fairly distracting, but he is also keen to observe the child. He moves from the entrance hall to the door of the consulting-room in order to keep both mother and child in view. While it seems to him that the mother is intruding into Matilde's space at the moment of saying goodbye, the child herself appears unconcerned; on the contrary, there is a moment of liveliness in the room, and Matilde moves slowly along the edge of the table, which is scattered with some of the toys that had been used and abandoned during the session. The child then turns her back on both analyst and mother and starts caressing the dolls, then handling them with firmer gestures, uttering as she does so a soft murmur—sounds, sighs, words spoken in an undertone. Something is happening, a game is begun, but the analyst cannot see what she is doing. Indeed, Matilde seems to exploit the moment so as to play, while protecting her experience from the analyst's attention, which he now understands to have been too active, just as the mother's had been.

This inevitably incomplete clinical vignette highlights the issue of possession in relation to play within the analytic context: whom does the playing belong to, who uses it? This is a question that tends to be blurred by the inevitable connection between child analysis and play—a connection that is predominantly clinical and technical but is also part of the historical development of the analysis of children. While playing belongs to the child, it is also shared with the analyst. But both the emphasis on playing as a tool for accessing the child's inner world (externalized or projected into the clinical space) and the idea of playing as the place of meeting and co-operation between analyst and child tend to put the onus onto the analyst, who watches and interprets as a way of establishing emotional contact with the child. But if we also take into consideration the *subjective experience* of the individual, the process of *experiencing*, then child analysis can be seen as creating, by providing a transitional area for play, the possibility for a potential experience of the self.

From this viewpoint, *play belongs to the child alone*, something asserted by Matilde after a session characterized by a polite but persistent avoidance of communication on her part, and by an equally polite but persistent soliciting of communication on the part of the analyst. The child then uses her own playing for the purpose of creating an experience—that of playing in the container of the analytical space when it has finally been left free for her to do so. We could even say that here it is the child who *makes use* of the analyst, oedipally engaged in a primal scene with her mother, in order to have a creative experience of herself as person and individual.

Naturally, the analyst also seeks to understand how what happened in the session with Matilde relates to him in terms of communication, since the very avoidance of communication can in itself be construed as a kind of communication. By shifting the perspective slightly, however, one can just as legitimately say that what happens is *the child's communication with a part of herself*, which is another way of describing the kind of experience intrinsic to playing.

Matilde's play takes shape *on the threshold*, in a transitional space–time where she appropriates something—in this case, the external event of a dialogue between mother and analyst—and uses it in the service of an aspect of her internal world. All of which demonstrates the transitional nature of playing. We are here touching upon the Winnicottian distinction between "play" and "playing". Winnicott writes:

> This area of playing is not inner psychic reality. It is outside the individual, but it is not the external world. Into this play area the child gathers objects or phenomena from external reality and uses them in the service of some sample derived from inner or personal reality. *Without hallucinating* the child puts out a sample of *dream potential* and lives with this sample in a chosen setting of fragments from external reality. In playing the child manipulates external phenomena *in the service of the dream* and invests chosen external phenomena with *dream meaning and feeling*. [1971b, p. 60, emphasis added]

According to Milner, just as dreaming at night is necessary to protect sleep, so the mental state of *reverie*, or day-dreaming, is necessary to protect creative wakefulness. In Winnicott's theory, as in Milner's, playing and dreaming are located in a continuum as potential self-experiences.

Dreaming as self-knowing

The story of *Alice in Wonderland* begins thus:

> Alice was beginning to get very tired of sitting by her sister on the bank, and of having nothing to do: once or twice she had peeped into the book her sister was reading, but it had no pictures or conversations in it, "and what is the use of a book," thought Alice "without pictures or conversation?" So she was considering in her own mind (as well as she could, for the hot day made her feel very sleepy and stupid), whether the pleasure of making a daisy-chain would be worth the trouble of getting up and picking the daisies, when suddenly a White Rabbit with pink eyes ran close by her.

Alice finds herself with a sister/mother who offers her no time or space for spontaneous use of her creative imagination. Alice's boredom expresses a feeling of emptiness and lack. The heat enveloping her is an allusion to the surfacing of confused and vague emotions that are not transformed into thought. Alice is in a state of both waiting and seeking; she is all potential wishing. In this moment of unconscious perplexity, which Winnicott (1941) termed "hesitation" and Milner "indeterminate thinking", the task of attention is to wait and "be content with being a frame, holding the empty space if something new is to emerge, something that has never been before" (1952a, p. 82).

Alice makes no attempt to fill this empty space, nor does she link together the stirring feelings and sensations by making a daisy-chain, which could itself be read metaphorically as the grasping of a particular and logical thought, or as the kind of reasoning that, in Milner's words (1957), may "work very well for managing the inanimate material environment . . . but does not work so well for understanding and managing the inner world" (p. 228). In the event, Alice *dreams*. The first character she meets is the White Rabbit, a watch in his waistcoat pocket, running because he is late. He puts in motion a psychic process and represents a *link* between the real world and the world of dreams and fantasies.

Alice follows the rabbit, enters his warren, and *falls* into a very deep well (similar to *falling* asleep), with the feeling that she is going through the earth down to the "Antipathies". She thus immerses herself in the dream world, the place "to which we can go in our sleep when we can turn our attention fully to the internal world" (Melzer, 1983). Alice enters the logic of the unconscious and of dream-work, organized by altered space and time, inverted perspective, ambiguity, and non-sense. Her journey in this "wonderland"—itself like an expanding universe generated by the child's imaginative elaboration—is described in Lewis Carroll's narrative with those poetical modes of expression that are typical of dreams and that, as Ella Sharpe stressed in 1937, employ the multiple aesthetic forms of simile, metaphor, metonymy, alliteration, and onomatopoeia.

The richness and complexity of Alice's journey in wonderland allude to the dream and its structure, but also to the potential of dreaming. Alice's dreaming shows that the dream is not only the compensatory fulfilment of a wish (the child fills her sense of emptiness and boredom), but it also describes the possibility of experiencing those dimensions of the self and of relating to others that are disturbed and conflictual. Dreaming allows Alice, almost an adolescent, to experience the loss of her identity in the continuous changes in the size of her body, in the size of the environment around her, in her conversations with herself, in the questions she asks the animals she meets. This encounter with the self, experienced as if through a telescope and oscillating from grandiose, manic situations to total helplessness, forces Alice to ask herself who she is while inducing a feeling of apprehension, confusion, bewilderment. Certain aspects of depression and death anxiety also surface during her journey—for example, in the sea of tears, where the miniature child and the tiny animals are afraid of drowning and from which they emerge all wet, or in the behaviour of the various animals she talks to, or in her meetings with other characters, especially the Queen of Hearts. At other points, Alice gets in touch with her aggression. Talking to the rat and the birds of her cat, Dinah, who is so good at "hunting", she provokes in them both fear and flight. Her aggression is expressed most explicitly perhaps when she throws the Rabbit out of the window, because, for the umpteenth time, he ignores her and takes her for the maid.

Alice's dream represents the problem of non-communication, or the incongruity of communication in dialogues where non-sense prevails: all of the characters continue their own monologues, act in an idiosyncratic way, and take no heed of the others. On the other hand, might not this prevalence of verbal nonsense express, as Milner (1942) says, "the relief of escaping from the false dominion of words which have acquired an absolute value, no longer functioning as a bridge between internal and external reality?" (p. 30)

Alice's dream is a metaphor filled with evocations. It describes that "geography of the mind" which involves, as Meltzer would say (1983), the possibility of living in different worlds, of visiting regions (of the self and of objects) whose inhabitants may not understand each other—hence the nonsense—because indigenous languages have different reference systems. It also alludes to the dimension of the dream as "theatre", where different scenarios open up and different characters appear and are incorporated into the narrative (Ferro, 1992).

But Alice's dream also evokes a further metaphoric dimension that we will now develop. Here the dream is like a journey, where the focus is not only on the regions and the inhabitants that one meets and gets to know but, most of all, on the process of journeying. The journey itself, the dreaming, is a path to knowledge: in fact, Alice's curiosity leads her to encounter the foreign and unknown parts of herself. As Milner (1975) says, "dreaming experience is to do with knowing who, what, one is, it is a testimony of states of being" (p. 278). In this context, dreaming is a kind of experience whose "full course" can be "allowed" (Winnicott, 1941, p. 67); as such, it is a search for, and an experience of, the self. Inherent in the narrative structure of Alice's journey in Wonderland is that element of "surprise to herself" which, in Winnicott's paradoxical way of describing subjective experience, is the unexpected, unforeseen self-revelation of the true self.

In one of the last lines of the tale, Alice exclaims, on waking: "Oh, I've had such a curious dream!" When she has finished telling the story, her sister kisses her and says: "It certainly *WAS* a curious dream, dear", stressing, with the use of the past tense, which is italicized in the text, an experience that has been realized and completed.

Acting out versus the experience of dreaming in the analytic situation

"I'm afraid . . . I'm gay"—with intense emotion in his voice, his face flushed and looking down, "Virgilio" starts his analysis, after the short embarrassed silence that marked the first few minutes of his first session. He is 15 years old, tall, pleasant-looking, very elegant, and well-groomed in an unconventional way.

That initial "I'm afraid"—so explosively emotive, and loaded with fear of a threat to an as-yet-undiscovered identity—is very soon replaced, in the first session, and in the immediately subsequent phases of the analysis, by calmer verbal descriptions: "I think", "I feel", "I sense I am gay".

From the start, Virgilio's analysis can be categorized as a problem of identification/de-identification: to be like his father and to be different from him, while avoiding the risk of a confusion with his mother. This is the background setting for the transference in the early phases of the analysis.

What seemed to Virgilio an increasingly irresistible homosexual inclination was centred on a dark, green-eyed, somewhat taller peer, "Maurizio", who represented both object and proof of this inclination. Virgilio recounted that they had tried mutual masturbation, which had left him deeply troubled and anxious; he spoke of his jealousy that Maurizio went out with girls; he described his efforts to steal Maurizio's underwear in the gym to use it fetishistically. These accounts stimulated interpretative comments from the analyst, focused primarily on the "point of view of the relationship". The most evident effect of this seemed to be to give the analyst the part of a "character" in the therapeutic relationship. He represented too close or too differentiated an object, "too much of an object", and this forced Virgilio to include him (the analyst) as an object of the transference, displacing elsewhere the need for individuation and recognition he had brought at the beginning. The "I'm afraid of being gay" risked taking the form of initiating homosexual—or, at least, sexualized—acts as a possible way of living his own conflicts about his identity, as a way of finding it. The desire to act on his feelings led Virgilio to form a troubled but firm resolution to take advantage of a projected school outing to propose a proper homosexual experience to Maurizio, during which he could finally "touch that exciting, disturbing body with his hands". These intentions are conveyed, "intimated", to the analyst and then experienced in a dream, which has become possible only because the analyst's attention has shifted from the content of the analysis to the broader picture. By the analyst's stepping back from this condition of being "too much an object" at this stage of the analysis, the conditions were created through which the boy could experience something in himself without acting it out.

At the beginning of his second year of analysis, during the first session in the week, right before the school outing, Virgilio says:

> I dreamt I was at Maurizio's, in his bathroom. It wasn't quite his bathroom, but it looked like it. The room was as large as this [pointing to the consulting-room], but different [he looks around as if to find inspiration]; let's say it was shaped like an upside-down U [again with a careful gesture of his hands he points at two virtually symmetrical rooms to be imagined at the end of the longer wall]. The strange thing is that it was like a bathroom made from mine and Maurizio's: there were two bathtubs, two sinks, everything was double. Odd, eh? We were both naked and we were taking a shower, but it was as if I was standing in front of a mirror which reflected him inside my bathroom . . . and I realized that I was him . . .

The discovery of his identity through his mirroring in the other seems to have been made possible by the creation of a *space* (the bathroom/consulting-room) where the dream could be dreamed. The *unexpected* representation of his self can obviously also be read in terms of a mirror transference with the analyst, who is seeing him *vis-à-vis* his therapy.

What can be highlighted in this dream is an acquisition in individual ego development, a capacity for subjective experiencing in a dream space with the qualities of a transitional space (the consulting-room as the bathroom of both Virgilio and Maurizio). The analytic scenario is the backdrop, the *precondition* for Virgilio's intimacy with himself, experienced internally, rather than acted out through staged homosexual behaviour.

From Milner's perspective, we can say that, in this moment of analysis, Virgilio's dream does not represent a symbolic text to be interpreted but is, rather, an attempt at symbolization which makes it possible to work on the manifest content without considering it necessarily a distortion of the latent content (1975, p. 344).

From the clinical point of view, one of the most significant implications of the developments in the understanding of the dream—begun, in the tradition of Winnicott and Milner, by Masud Khan (1962, 1972, 1976)—is that a missing or faulty acquisition of the dream space, the space where the dream process takes place, can involve the tendency to act out the latent content: the dream is thus enacted in object relationships in social space. In Khan's account of the "good dream", the use of dream space is similar to the use of transitional space offered by a blank sheet of paper for a child to draw on. Dream space is an achievement of the developmental process of personalization that is facilitated by the experience of maternal support and care.

The sense of non-sense: playing the trauma, dreaming the trauma, and the use of the analytic space

During the first phase of her analysis, while busy drawing or making things out of clay for her mother, 7-year-old "Silvia" frequently says: "If there's some time left, I play." The sentence is uttered in passing, rather like a fragment of an internal musing, said out loud, part of a discourse with herself. Sometimes at the end of the session, in a tone of sadness and irritation, she says: "I wasted all my time doing this little work for Mummy, but I am happy." For a time, this "little work" for Mummy, having to work for Mummy, is the configuration that crystallizes, almost concretely, the child's psychic experience in analysis. It is this mode of communication, together with the frequent and elaborate drawings, always tidy, conventional, that alerts the analyst to Silvia's inability to separate, to get free of her mother, whom she sees as fragile, needy, deprived, an object demanding her attention and life-giving care.

For Silvia at this point the sessions seem to be almost a ritual, an opportunity for getting those things that she lacks but has to get to pass on to her mother. The analyst [MDR] is idealized as the source of these things: attention, availability, vitality. The child's own vitality seems constrained. Coming and going between analyst and mother, like a water-carrier bringing nourishment from the former to the latter, she has no space or time for herself.

The words "If there's time left, I play" offer an insight into the limiting nature of the manic defence for the child's self. This enables the analyst to interpret some of the issues and gradually open up a subsequent phase where Silvia seems more capable of finding a space–time for her own play.

Every once in a while a new element of pleasure in playing emerges, corresponding in the analyst's countertransference to a livelier, more attentive interest in the scenes the child now risks representing. This is a phase in which the analyst, besides supporting and facilitating Silvia's emerging capacity to play, can also share in the issues and sometimes identify and suggest transference links.

In the emerging of Silvia's capacity to play, a limit and an obstacle can be observed that lies in the fact that the full course of the experience is not allowed. There is a sudden suspension of playing, something that took the analyst by surprise the first time it occurred: the sequence is interrupted, the scenario crumbles, the plot loses its sense of direction. Silvia's interest and engagement dry up; occasionally the toys she holds drop from her hands. Moments of confusion and disorientation follow as the child moves from a state of well-organized, articulated play, in which she connects with the analyst, to a suspension of her emotional and cognitive abilities, in which she becomes detached a and falls into a sort of torpor or sleepiness.

These "gaps" in Silvia's mental functioning do not always find an emotional correspondence in the analyst's countertransference, suggesting that they are not linked to the configuration or nuances of the analytic relationship in that moment. Rather, the analyst frequently feels that she is a witness to a sudden, inexplicable interruption in the contact between her and the child, but, even more, between the child and herself. The analyst is confronted with a "break", a "gap", that at the moment it is happening cannot be given an interpretation, because the child for whom this might be useful is not, in any real sense, present. Instead, the break must simply be accepted in the countertransference.

It seems that it is precisely this availability of the analyst to "take" this sudden "sea change", to support the break—increasingly through recourse to her imaginative faculties—that provides the child with a sort of "place" where presence and absence, contact and detachment, and the very "fall" from one state to the other can form part of a cohesive unity of space–time.

The increasing awareness of establishing this dimension allows Silvia to begin to *incorporate what had been the interruption and limit of the playing into the playing itself*. The game scenario begins to develop and becomes coloured by new emotions: the farm where the animals live and act, or the house where the family reside, are suddenly overwhelmed by a storm or hurricane that rips the roof off (symbolizing the head, the thoughts, not only of herself and her mother, but also—in the transference—of the analyst); the cow and calf who leave the confines of the fence to venture out into the meadow are swept up by a whirlwind that separates them and causes the calf to stumble and fall into a ravine. Similarly, in the recurrent playing at families, when the mother is attending to her child, the baby falls from her high-chair or from her bed whenever the mother suddenly turns her back or leaves. In these episodes, where the *fall is played*, the feelings of anxiety, fear, helplessness, and getting lost can emerge and be experienced.

From this particular perspective, there are striking similarities between this phase of Silvia's analysis and certain aspects of the analysis of another patient, "Leopoldo", a 16-year-old with marked schizoid traits. During his second year of treatment he begins to interrupt and suspend communication, withdrawing into lengthy silences, lying on the couch like an inanimate object, putting a distance, an insuperable barrier between himself and his analyst. This tends to occur at the point where a more spontaneous, emotionally engaged dialogue has begun, creating an expectation of a further development in the relationship. The subsequent break would leave the analyst feeling disillusioned and somewhat depressed.

The analyst feels Silvia's sudden "sea change" as the re-enactment, in the analytic setting, of the toddler's reaction to the impingement represented by her mother's sudden mood changes, and the consequent drop in attention and emotional interest in her.

In the same way, the "change in climate" in Leopoldo's session is understood, through the shifts in the countertransference, as the re-enactment of another specific emotional situation: maternal depression and the son's infantile mirroring of it.

The boy's withdrawal not only demonstrates the anxiety he feels in relation to his dependence on, and emotional surrender to, the object, but it is also an expression of his compulsion to repeat, in the transference, the fending off of the object in an effort to master the trauma of abandonment and loss. It further indicates the extent of Leopoldo's identification with his depressed mother (Green's "dead mother", 1983), who is transformed from a source of life into a mute, colourless, inaccessible figure. Above all, the interruption in communication re-enacts the traumatic childhood event of a "break" both in the object relationship and in the self, a "drop" in the object cathexis which creates a void that cannot be filled by representation, an "amputation" of the vital potential of the self.

Through the transference, the analyst senses how Leopoldo's "turning off" of his emotional presence and Silvia's retreat into lethargy derive from the fear of expressing emotions they found to be violent, overwhelming, uncontrollable. They also share the common anxiety that the mother's depression, the withdrawal of her function of support and containment, was actually a consequence of their own needs, drives, and feelings.

For both Silvia and Leopoldo, the experience of the continuing presence of an analyst who is capable of "bearing the situation", who can hold the "fall" and the "void" and can "survive the collapse" within the on-going space–time of the analytic process, is essential. The analyst also continues to try to re-animate the broken relationship by making use of her own imaginative faculties and continuing to interpret processes as carefully and tactfully as possible. This encourages a movement away from a literal relational space, from a state of the self where these events just happen, to an internal space that can include these events and facilitate an emotional experience that can be represented through dreaming.

A few months after beginning analysis, in a session at the beginning of the week, Leopoldo relates a dream he had the night before which also contains a transference communication:

> "It's odd, I'm so used to going to the mountains and yet I dreamt about falling . . . *I was climbing a mountain, but I didn't have the right gear, my clothes weren't warm enough, the path was difficult . . . there was even some ice, the ground was slippery, I felt I could hardly stand, I tried to go on, I could see the cabin I had to reach further up . . . the shrubs I tried to hold on to were no good because they didn't have deep enough roots. Suddenly, I fell . . . I was falling into the void."*

Throughout the course of his analysis, Leopoldo would take the opportunity to continue the internal experience embarked upon in this dream. In the ensuing phases he would dream of falling many times, but the staging of the dream became richer and more articulated. New features characterized the mountainous environment, and other characters, such as his child self, appear; an adolescent Leopoldo carries him on his shoulders, or holds his hand on the ascent. A child to hold and support, but also to let fall at a certain point, when he had become a burden, a limit, an obstacle to growth. Other figures included a fellow walker, the analyst-guide, whose presence is acknowledged or ignored, avoided or used, according to the different alternating levels of psychic functioning and to the emotional configuration of the relationship.

In general terms, what we have been stressing here is that, from our particular perspective, the space where Silvia's playing can unwind and run its full course, where Leopoldo's dream can be dreamed, is a space where both patients first experience what has already happened in the past, through the non-sense of clinical material which has been accepted and contained. It cannot properly be described in terms of shared space, in that there is still, at this stage, no joint determination of meanings. Rather, we are here in the process of establishing a *potential space*, a space made available for use, where traumatic events that could not previously be experienced can then be included and integrated into the play or the dream, themselves part of that experiencing process. In this way, the traumas can finally assume a *personal and idiomatic* emotional meaning for the self.

CHAPTER SEVEN

To unravel unhappiness

W. H. Auden

A Life of One's Own. By Joanna Field. Chatto and Windus. 7s. 6d.

This is a remarkable and, I think, important book. It is best described as a record of auto-analysis, a detailed account of a series of experiments in minor psychotherapy. The first important thing about the book is that the author was not a "case"; she was a lecturer in academic psychology, had many friends, and early in the experiment became happily married; i.e. she is a perfectly ordinary example of the middle-class educated and intelligent woman who has to earn her living and is quite capable of looking after herself and getting on with other people of both sexes—no better and no worse than nine-tenths of the people one knows.

One day she realised that she was unhappy and decided to do something about it. That is the second important point. Nine-

This review appeared in *The Listener*, 28 November 1934. *A Life of One's Own* (London, 1934) was written by Marion Milner under the name Joanna Field.

tenths of the people one knows either do not consciously realise that they are unhappy—and by unhappiness I do not mean sudden fits of acute misery or depression like the aftermath of 'flu, but that dull unrelenting pressure to which people, like those who live within earshot of a waterfall, grow so accustomed that they take it for granted—or if they do realise it for a moment, are afraid and thrust away the unpleasant idea, drugging themselves with work, parties or what not. Its presence in a neighbour even superficial observation will detect, but to admit it in oneself is so damaging to one's self-conceit, except to those to whom it is their sole luxury, that such admission is rare.

Miss Field set out first to discover the nature and objects of this unhappiness and then its remedy. The technique of discovery is nothing very new and exciting now: free association writing, either off the reel or on a set subject, automatic drawings, catching the wandering thought of the moment and putting it into words, transcribing dreams and so on. But the results were as startling to the subject as they would be to any of us who choose to apply them. She imagined herself intelligent, rational, civilised, believing in intellectual progress, and the experiments revealed her to herself as timid, desperately anxious about the effect she was having on other people, full of sly equivocations and tricks, hysterically violent and irrational in her judgments when her self was threatened, and at a deeper level terrified, terrified of the future and of the point of existence, of her instinctive self, and of God as the avenger and punisher.

I do not know if Miss Field is acquainted with the work of Homer Lane, but everything she says is a striking confirmation of his teaching. He used to say that the first question you should ask a patient is his opinion of God. Our way of bringing up children, by a combination of moral commands, forgiveness, penances and punishments—the Pharisaic law implants in the unconscious a guilty hatred of God as he is consciously presented to us, and is responsible for those errors on which Blake so unerringly put his finger: "(1) That Man has two real existing principles—a Body and a Soul. (2) That Energy called evil is alone from the Body; and that Reason, called good, is alone from the Soul. (3) That God will torment Man in eternity for following his energies." The consequence of such beliefs is that man is divided against himself, and the energies or instincts are not allowed to develop beyond the infantile possessive level; i.e. that he can never be self-forgetful. Of this possessive personal unconsciousness dominated by automatic thinking, Miss Field gives a searching and devastating analysis. She does not say much about her childhood, perhaps wisely. She refused to undergo psychoanalysis, feeling it was not quite playing the game. Few people have the time or money for it, and one ought to be able to discover a method which one can work oneself, taking the forgotten incidents of childhood as given, and working from the present.

It would be unfair to her book, which is as exciting as a detective story, to give away all the methods she tried, but they included both physical and mental exercises, the former paralleling in an interesting way the work of Mr Matthias Alexander. She found that the first, hardest, and most essential task was to learn to relax that physical and mental rigidity to which we all become habituated.

> What, then, was entirely under the control of my will? It seemed that the only thing that was even potentially so controlled was my attention. I could not control what I saw when I looked in a certain direction, but I could at least control what direction I should look in. . . . It had also been one of my greatest discoveries that when I could not attend as I wished, then I must deliberately turn my attention loose and let it lead me to the distracting cause. . . . Selfishness is not usually a failure of will, it is not that one deliberately sees a selfish and an unselfish attitude and chooses the selfish. It is that one is selfish because one unwittingly indulges in a kind of thinking, which cannot, by its very nature, recognise the realness of other people's needs.

Secondly, that—unacceptable as it may be to those who earn their living by it—academic knowledge, logical comprehension of ideas in books were quite useless, indeed, more often than not, even a form of escape. Thirdly—and this throws some light on literature—that the expression of thought in words, becoming aware of it, was the beginning of a process of development and enrichment.

> In perceiving the external world the effort to express what I saw invariably brought rich results. Often, when vaguely

> bored in a restaurant or the street, it would be enough to say, for instance: "That man looks like a pig", and at once I would find he had become alive. . . .

And, lastly, that the unconscious is not only the refuge of childish phantasies and fears, but a source of creative wisdom; there is an instinctive sense of living, if it is trusted; a trust, however, quite different from blind irrationalism.

One is tempted again and again to quote passages for their richness of insight, but quotation could not do justice to the sustained interest of Miss Field's story which culminates in a mystical experience.

The last chapter of interpretation is, inevitably, less interesting, but the author would be the last to claim it as important. I doubt whether speaking of male and female elements explains anything. If there are both elements in every individual, neither can be sacrificed without damage—the Gretchen is as unsatisfactory as the school teacher.

A Life of One's Own is an account of the unhappiness of the average person, and of methods to overcome it which could be employed by anyone, provided they have the patience and the courage of the experimenter. Such qualities, unfortunately, especially the first, are rare, but this book should do much to stimulate them.

CHAPTER EIGHT

Critical notice of *On Not Being Able to Paint*

D. W. Winnicott

Let no one think that this book is just about painting or not painting. Yet it had to have its title because in that way the writing of the book started. The real purpose of the book only becomes clear to the author in the course of her experience of writing, in fact the book is itself an example of its main theme. This theme, which gradually becomes clear to the reader, is foreshadowed in an early quotation: "Concepts can never be presented to me merely, they must be knitted into the structure of my being, and this can only be done through my own activity" (M. P. Follett, *Creative Experience*).

The central concept which is presented to the reader and apprehended by the writer through the writing of the book has to do with the subjective way of experiencing and the role of this in creative process. Thus the book is in one sense a plea for the rec-

This review appeared in the *British Journal of Medical Psychology* in 1951. *On Not Being Able to Paint* (London: Heinemann, 1951) was written by Marion Milner under the name Joanna Field.

ognition of subjectivity as having its own place and way of functioning, just as legitimate and as necessary as objectivity, but different. As applied to education, it is pointed out that subjectivity must be understood by teachers, otherwise the objectivity aimed at must be in danger of fatal distortion. Painting comes in as a jumping-off place; it was the surprise of discovering the power to make "free" drawings that concentrated the writer's attention on this problem of subjectivity or subjective action.

The concept of the role of subjectivity which emerges has two main aspects, one to do with illusion, the other with spontaneity. Both are connected with what the writer calls the interplay of differences, out of which creativity proceeds, but if interplay is to be allowed in oneself one must be prepared for mental pain. Such an interplay needs various descriptions according to the level being considered. At a comparatively late stage of emotional development, what is familiar in psycho-analytic literature about unconscious conflict between love and hate in interpersonal relationships is relevant, and indeed this paved the way for all other statements. Such conflict involves the problem of the preservation of the loved object from hate and from erotic attacks (whether in fact or in fantasy) and creation is seen in this setting as an act of reparation. If one considers earlier stages in emotional development of the individual, one must use other language, such as the statement that magical creativity is an alternative to magical annihilation.

If I understand the author aright she wishes to make a yet more fundamental statement about creativity. She wishes to say that it results from what is for her (and perhaps for everyone) the primary human predicament. This predicament arises out of the non-identity of what is conceived of and what is to be perceived. To the objective mind of another person seeing from outside, that which is outside an individual is never identical with what is inside that individual. But there can be, and must be, for health (so the writer implies), a meeting place, an overlap, a stage of illusion, intoxication, transfiguration. In the arts this meeting place is pre-eminently found through the medium, that bit of the external world which takes the form of the inner conception. In painting, writing, music, etc., an individual may find islands of peace and so get momentary relief from the primary predicament of healthy human beings.

Psycho-analysts are accustomed to thinking of the arts as wish-fulfilling escapes from the knowledge of this discrepancy between inner and outer, wish and reality. It may come as a bit of a shock to some of them to find a psycho-analyst drawing the conclusion, after careful study, that this wish-fulfilling illusion may be the essential basis for all true objectivity. If these moments of fusion of subject and object, inner and outer, are indeed more than islands of peace, then this fact has very great importance for education. For what is illusion when seen from outside is not best described as illusion when seen from inside; for that fusion which occurs when the object is felt to be one with the dream, as in falling in love with someone or something, is, when seen from inside, a psychic reality for which the word illusion is inappropriate. For this is the process by which the inner becomes actualised in external form and as such becomes the basis, not only of internal perception, but also of all true perception of environment. Thus perception itself is seen as a creative process. In practice psycho-analysts, just like other people, love the arts and value the work of those who traffic in illusion. This book is showing psychoanalysts a way in which they may bring their theory into line not only with their psychotherapy but also with their daily lives.

Moreover the author is reminding psycho-analysts and all teachers that teaching is not enough; each student must create what is there to be taught, and so arrive at each stage of learning in his own way. If he temporarily forgets to acknowledge debts this is easily forgiven, since in place of paying debts he re-discovers with freshness and originality and also with pleasure, and both the student and the subject grow in the experience.

The second thread of the book, the role of spontaneity in creativeness, is also something that analysts tend to allow for more in their practice than in their theory They are well used to theorising about the effects of too rigid control of spontaneity, imposed in the interests of social living and propriety. What they, and also other teachers, are less used to considering is the stultifying effect on the creative spirit of too great insistence not just on propriety but on objectivity. This insistence on objectivity concerns not only perception but also action, and creativity can be destroyed by too great insistence that in acting one must know beforehand what one is doing.

CHAPTER NINE

On Robinson Crusoe's island

Margaret Walters

About thirty years ago, I came across a shabby, second-hand copy of one of those old blue-and-white Pelicans. It was called *A Life of One's Own* (1934), and I was hooked from the moment I started; I read it, and read it over and over again. A great many other people, I discovered later, had the same reaction. I remember looking curiously at the small black-and-white jacket photograph of the author, Joanna Field—a well-brought up, give-nothing-away English face. (It must have been one of the worst photographs ever taken of Marion.) But Joanna Field's voice was immediately riveting: direct flexible and suggestive; it ranged with unembarrassed ease from the most apparently trivial detail to the most serious philosophic speculations.

Marion Milner herself described that first book as the record of "a seven years' study of living to find out what kinds of experience made me happy". (She had already done a degree in psychology at London University, studied in the United States with the industrial psychologist Elton Mayo, and conducted a lengthy survey in girls' public schools in England which was published as "The Human Problem in Schools". It has never been reprinted, but for all its rather dated methodology, its attempt to distinguish when and why the girls were bored and dull, and when they seemed to come to life, and follow, freely, their deeper interests, does foreshadow what would become Marion's dominant interests.) While she was doing this work, Milner began to feel, very acutely, "the gap between knowing and living". So her aim in *A Life of One's Own* is straightforward, if not simple: she sets out to discover what made her feel happy, or unhappy. She wants to map what she calls "the no man's land which lay between the dark kingdom of the psychoanalyst and the cultivated domains of my conscious thought". And she will start from scratch, taking nothing at all for granted: using her diaries, making lists of her likes and dislikes, she carefully catches and observes her moods, of boredom or of pleasure. One of the things that amused and delighted me, even on that first reading, was her choice of quotations for chapter headings. Some are predictable enough. She cites the mystic Lao-Tse several times, the naturalist Gilbert White—a wonderful passage about the coming and going of birds on a summer evening—and once, very tellingly, that great introspective essayist Montaigne: "We are great fools. 'He has passed his life in idleness,' we say, or 'I have done nothing today.' What? Have you not lived? That is not only the fundamental, but the most industrious of all your occupations. Have you known how to take repose, you have done more than he who has taken cities and empires." It was Montaigne, Marion once wrote, who when she first read him in 1926, inspired her to keep a diary.

But it is typical of Marion that she turns most often to a very unexpected source—to the daylight world of Daniel Defoe's *Robinson Crusoe*, using his efforts to survive to map her own very different quest. Through the book, we glimpse the shipwrecked sailor anxiously viewing this unknown country and miserably acknowledging that he is marooned on an island; we see him taking pot-shots at the wildlife and trying to decide which plants might be edible. He falls ignominiously into deep water, and he nearly drowns as he searches his wrecked ship for useful goods. We share his sleepless nights, full of terrors as he imagines lurking enemies, and we share his delight at unexpectedly discovering blades of green-springing barley on a rubbish tip.

There is a lively wit, I have always thought—and a wit characteristic of Marion—in this deft use of a story about physical survival as a map for her exploration of the inner life. Moreover, I think that it is important that Marion chose a child's story—or at least a story that has been appropriated by children. And a story that girls love just as much as boys—partly, I think, because we recognize the hero's plight. Isolated on his island, the "hero" is essentially passive, and his most strenuous efforts to survive amount to little more than a form of—housekeeping.

And Marion's witty and thoughtful use of Defoe hints at some of her most engaging qualities, ones that she retained until the day she died—her capacity for childlike clarity and directness (though that childlike quality, of course, was accompanied by considerable sophistication); her femininity, in the sense that she knows when she has to accept circumstances and simply wait, observing the often baffling workings of her mind; and her pragmatism, her coolly practical way of approaching even the darker recesses of the human mind.

Her exploration of the "no man's land" between psychoanalysis and everyday thinking is couched simply and directly. At times, her prose achieves an almost scientific detachment: she observes her shifting moods with a cool detachment, noting down her vague discontents and equally vague spells of optimism, tracing flashes of pleasure of boredom or anger to their sources. Her techniques are various: she makes lists, of "things I hate" and "things I love"; she tries free-associating, in writing, to make up her mind about a man "who half attracted, half repelled me"; she experiments to find out how she might enjoy looking at paintings or listening to music and discovers internal gestures that seem to work—"Last Wednesday I went to the opera at Covent Garden, *Rigoletto*. I was dead tired and could not listen at first, sitting on the miserably cramped gallery benches, but then I remembered to put myself out of myself, close to the music—and sometimes it closed over my head, and I came away rested, feeling light-limbed." Later, when she is thinking about marriage, she makes a little sketch of her inner landscape that helps her make up her mind. As the book progresses, she experiments with and analyses meticulously the "forces distorting and limiting my powers of perception" and patiently experiments with ways of controlling them. (On second and third readings, it becomes clear that, among other things, *A Life of One's Own* is a careful experiment; indeed, she picked up and deliberately used that word in the title of her next book, *An Experiment in Leisure* [1986].)

In *A Life of One's Own,* Marion moves easily between apparently trivial concerns—she worries about a new haircut, she envies a friend's fashionable clothes, tries hard to convince a new acquaintance "that I'm not so innocent as I look". I say apparently trivial: part of her genius as writer and analyst was that no detail, however minor, ever seemed trivial. Her prose shifts gracefully between everyday living on the one hand, and life-determining problems: Should she marry? Should she have a child? How should she work? The book was the fruit of seven years of patient introspection and diary-keeping. She discovered that the simple act of looking inwards, of patiently waiting on her fleeting feelings, then naming them somehow became "a force which changed my whole being". She demonstrated the effect in one of the most beautiful, and also most characteristic, passages in *A Life of One's Own.* She was on holiday in the Black Forest in Germany, the weather was bad, her companion was "nervously ill", and she felt thoroughly bored, irritated, and depressed—until she tried her technique of simply naming what she saw:

> "I said, I see a white house with red geraniums and I hear a child crooning. And this most simple incantation seemed to open a door between me and the world . . . those flickering leaf-shadows playing over the heap of grass, fresh scythed. The shadows are blue, I don't know which, but I feel them in my bones. Down into the shadows of the gully, across it through glistening space, space that hangs suspended filling the gully, so that little sounds wander there, lose themselves and are drowned, the air is full of sounds, sighs of wind in the trees, sighs which face back into the overhanging silence. A bee passes, a golden ripple in the quiet air. A chicken at my feet fussily crunches a blade of grass."

(I suspect, incidentally, that Shakespeare was lurking in the back of her mind when she wrote this; his rhythms—"the Island is full of noises, sounds and sweet airs"—seem to be briefly echoed in her own prose.) Passages like this have led some of her readers to describe her, and with some reason, as a mystic. But if she was a mystic—she remained sceptical about the term—any tendency to otherworldliness or to transcendence was tempered by her passionate concern with the precise details of the world around her. And she never lost her sense that that world existed in its own right, and not simply as a romantic mirror for human emotions.

An American friend once described her as a "body mystic"—and, with some reservations, she was prepared to accept that phrase, for most visionary writing never loses touch with the body; it is always, literally, earthed. Like the writers who influenced her, she passionately loves the physical world, in all its beauty and variety. In *An Experiment in Leisure,* Marion invoked, tellingly, one of the greatest English novelists, Emily Bronte: "Like Catherine Earnshaw of *Wuthering Heights,* I think I'd cry for earth if ever I found myself in heaven."

Marion seems to have discovered almost at once that sign of a real writer—a personal and distinctive voice of her own. She was impressively well-read in English literature, and I think that that early reading shaped her style and her thinking. Her taste seems to have ranged from classics like *Robinson Crusoe* to contemporary novelists like Aldous Huxley, from Shakespeare to Blake to T. S. Eliot. In her first seminar teaching for the Institute of Psycho-Analysis, she apparently—to the amused disapproval of Masud Khan, who was one of her pupils—used, instead of any analytic text, the English journalist and critic Christopher Caudwell's book *Illusion and Reality.*

The very first chapter of *A Life of One's Own* is preceded by that famous passage from Joseph Conrad's *Nostromo*:

> A man that is born falls into a dream like a man who falls into the sea. If he tries to climb out into the air as inexperienced people do, he drowns. No, I tell you! The way is to the destructive element submit yourself, and with the exertions of your hands and feet in the water make the deep, deep sea keep you up, in the destructive element immerse.

In fact, that particular quotation is even more relevant to Marion's second book, *An Experiment in Leisure,* which tries to come to terms with the darker side of human experience, with "the destructive element". She remarked, in her introduction, that it "could be called a study in the use of masochism". It is certainly a study in femininity—femininity as a responsive openness, a willingness to allow people, and things, and ideas to seize her imagination, to take her over for a time, at least. In *An Experiment in Leisure*, she takes a hard look at femininity at the point where it easily slides into perversion: as she remarks, "there are [people] who are less certain in their attitudes, who are often more aware of other people's identity than their own; for them, and very often they are women, it is so fatally easy to live parasitically upon other people's happiness, to answer the question—'What shall we do today?' by—'We'll do whatever you like, my dear'."

After the daylight world of *A Life of One's Own*, she does venture into the darkness, does have the courage to immerse herself in the destructive—or the self-destructive—element. And the book certainly contains a remarkably shrewd analysis of women who are "brought up to be nice, to be gentle and considerate—just those who tend to fall in love with men who are ruthless". She is clear-headed about the dangers of romantic love. "As long as your sense of the force that lives you is projected on to another person, then the continual presence of that person is utterly essential—without him life has no significance whatever. In spite of the verdict of romantic literature and the films I was certain that such a state could only be a phase; one cannot live parasitically on another person's life for ever, eventually one must face the other in oneself. . . ." She admits, sadly, that "this finding of self in oneself was perhaps harder for a woman than man".

In the course of those two early books, Marion emerged as a fully fledged writer, with a distinctive and confident voice of her own. She has developed a style—and, as an old fashioned literary critic, I believe that the style is the woman. Marion's prose is pragmatic, flexible, and imaginative, and it has been fed by a wide and discriminating reading in English literature: she is consciously, and knowledgeably, writing within a great literary tradition. So, for example, within a few pages in *An Experiment in Leisure*, meditating on death as physical reality and as psychic metaphor, she can invoke W. B. Yeats's remark that "an emotion does not exist till it has found its expression in colour or in sound or in form"; move on to the great sermon on death preached by John Donne at Whitehall in 1630, "that private and retired man that thought himself his own forever, and never came forth, must in the dust of his grave be published, and (such are the revolutions of the graves) be mingled with the dust of every highway and of every dunghill and swallowed in every puddle and pool." She continues by sympathetically quoting John Keats's confession that in a crowded room, "the identity of everyone begins to press upon me so that I am in a very little time annihilated—not only among men: it would be the same in a nursery of children". She finishes with a contemporary poet, T. S. Eliot (I sometimes find it hard to remember that she was a contemporary of his), writing on death, in a passage from *Ash Wednesday*. The book contains one of her first references to William Blake—a quotation that she says she discovered while she was reading Yeats's essays:

> I know of no other Christianity, and know of no other gospel, than the liberty, both of body and mind, to exercise the divine art of imagination, the real and eternal world of which this vegetable universe is but a faint shadow, and in which we shall live in our eternal or imaginative bodies when these vegetable mortal bodies are no more. What is the joy of heaven but improvement in the things of the spirit? What are the pains of Hell but ignorance, idleness, bodily list and the devastation of things of the spirit? Answer this for yourselves, and expel from amongst you those who pretend to despise the labours of art and science, which alone are the labours of the gospel. [Blake, "To the Christians", from *Jerusalem*]

Milner reaches for these English writers easily and naturally: these are the books that have formed her, the literature that has educated her and nourished her talent, that has enabled her to become, herself, a highly original writer—indeed, I think she became a major writer in a great English tradition.

I had been reading and re-reading *A Life of One' s Own* and *An Experiment in Leisure* for years before I first came across Marion Milner in the flesh. But in the 1980s I reviewed *Eternity's Sunrise* (1987a) for the World Service, and Miriam Newman invited me to a *Squiggle* meeting where Marion was going to read a passage from one of her papers. She must have been well into her 80s, still startlingly beautiful and vital (she seemed to have nothing in common with that conventional photo on the back of *A Life of One's*

Own—though I have come to suspect, since, that that respectable English gentlewoman was also a genuine and quite deep part of Marion's complicated personality). At the *Squiggle* meeting, she read few brief passages from her 1952 paper, "The Role of Illusion in Symbol Formation". What struck me then, and lingers with me still, was not so much the details of her interpretation, but the vivid reality with which she invokes her small patient marshalling his forces in his war games, and issuing orders to his analyst: "He says, 'You have got to bring all your people over to my village, the war is over.' I have to bring the animals and people over in trucks, but at once he says they must go back because they all have to watch the burning of the whole stack of matchboxes (which he has bought with his own money)." At a later stage, Marion continues, there were times "when he was stage managing and it was my imagination which caught fire. He would close the shutters of the room and insist that it be only candle light, sometimes a dozen candles arranged in patterns, or all grouped together in a solid block. And then he would make what he called furnaces . . . and often there had to be a sacrifice, a lead soldier had to be added to the fire and this figure was spoken of as either the victim or the sacrifice."

As Marion read aloud, it was as if a gap of nearly fifty years had been wiped out: she seemed a young woman again, and the small boy was almost uncannily present in the lecture hall. That case, Marion explained when she re-published it, was in fact supervised by Melanie Klein, and the paper was originally printed in an issue of the *International Journal of Psycho-Analysis* honouring Klein. But its power seems to owe comparatively little to Kleinian theory, or, for that matter, to any other version of psychoanalytic theory: it owes everything to Marion's imaginative sympathy and insight, and to her gift for catching complicated, highly ambiguous, emotional situations in simple, jargon-free language. Marion herself once said that the central idea of that whole paper was captured in a few lines: "The moments when the original poet in each of us created the outside world for us, by finding the familiar in the unfamiliar, are perhaps forgotten by most people; or else they are guarded in some secret place of memory because they were too much like visitations of the gods to be mixed with everyday thinking. But in autobiographies some do dare to tell, and often in poetry." Nobody but Marion could have thought, or written that; and, characteristically, Marion gives her poetic insight a simple, practical application, perhaps unconsciously but appositely using a buried image of light that echoed the case she had just described. "Perhaps in ordinary life, it is good teachers who are most aware of these moments, from outside, since it is their job so to stage-manage the situation that imagination catches fire and a whole subject or skill lights up with significance."

In a way, she seems to be hinting that sometimes the best role for the psychoanalyst is as a kind of stage manager. Her essay offers—as, of course, Winnicott did, many times, and more recently Christopher Bollas—the image of her consulting-room as a safe, transitional space, as a stage if you like, where creation becomes potential, becomes possible. But it is her prose style, with its distinctive rhythms, the turns of speech, that makes her a great analytic writer. Marion never seems to begin from theory; she begins from the person in front of her, working with what they say—and even more important do. Her case studies involve concrete objects—toys, or, of course, drawings. I have always been delighted by her 1955 paper, "The Communication of Primary Sensual Experience" (1987), in which she takes a patient's drawings—actually, some of Susan's—and does a poll on each one, asking for brief comments from analysts and art teachers, who are identified simply: Jungian, Kleinian, Anna Freudian, Independent (female), painter and art teacher (male). The exercise may not have been particularly rewarding in itself, but it is a wonderful and comic example of Marion's scepticism about theory. As any analyst must, she does use it, of course, but she is always aware that any theory must be provisional, that it must be tested again and again against reality and, if necessary, transformed. I would argue that Marion Milner became a major analyst because her prose—her sharp eye, her accurate ear, for the idiosyncratic life-giving detail—is constantly calling received truths into question. In her appendix to *On Not Being Able to Paint*, Marion set out to relate—or perhaps the correct word is translate—her personal experiments to psychoanalytic ideas about creativity; it stands as a fascinating exercise, but only an exercise undertaken after the real work is complete, a translation. And even here, she falls back on her own developed style. Take the passage where she talks about the time in the baby's life when "even the faculty of consciousness itself was felt to be entirely creative, to be aware of anything was simply to have made it"; she backs up her point not by invoking any psychoanalyst—not even Freud, that great prose stylist with whom I suspect Milner had far more in common than she had with Anna Freud or Klein—but one of her favourite English poets: "All one saw was one's own, as Traherne said, and it was one's own because one had made it."

Milner admits that she hesitated before using the word "symbol" in the book, because she felt confused by "the classical psycho-analytic attempt to restrict the use of the word to denoting only the defensive function of symbols"; only now, after she has followed through her own ideas, can she assert that:

> a work of art is necessarily and primarily a symbol. I could look on the artist as creating symbols for the life of feeling, creating ways in which the inner life may be made knowable, which, as Freud said, can only be done in terms of the outer life. . . . And since this inner life is the life of the body . . . in his concern for the permanence and immortality of his work, [the artist] is not only seeking to defy his own mortality (as analysts have said), he is perhaps also trying to convey something of the sense of timelessness which can accompany those moments . . . what the painter does conceptualize in non-verbal symbols, is the astounding experience of how it feels to be alive, the experience, known from inside, of being a moving, living body in space, with capacities to relate oneself to other objects in space. And included in this experience of being alive is the very experience of the creative process itself.

This is a remarkable and very complex statement, central to her work. If Marion was clarifying her own methods and perceptions, she was also challenging the psychoanalytic establishment—which, she remarked, perhaps has never had very much to say about "psychic creativeness". She hints here as well that theory easily hardens into jargon; unless it is constantly questioned, qualified, brought up against the immediate, the physical, the unexpected, it can become a strait-jacket. And Marion's best analytic writing is as idiosyncratic, as personal, and as challenging to received ideas as the rest of her work.

In fact, though she committed her life to it, Marion could take a healthily sceptical—indeed, very mischievous—attitude towards psychoanalytic orthodoxy. In the front room of her house in Provost Road—a calm and formal room, beautifully arranged with furniture and some paintings inherited from her mother (on that side of the family, Marion came from the landed gentry, and sometimes it showed). But on the wall nearest the door was hung a large painting of her own, a rather sumptuous canvas in varying shades of deep, dark, rich reds; in a way, it was a trick painting—at second glance, it arranged itself into farmyard scene: two hens aggressively confronting each other over a tiny egg. Marion would take any new visitor to look at the painting and then announce that it was about Melanie Klein and Anna Freud squabbling over who'd given birth to British Psycho-Analytical Society. Anyone who failed to laugh, or at least smile, had a certain amount of ground to make up.

Marion, a great original, had most in common with that other original, D. W. Winnicott, and the two became close friends. Two of the most shrewdly entertaining papers published in that wonderful collection, *The Suppressed Madness of Sane Men*, are about D. W. Winnicott; in one of them, she marvellously, and unexpectedly, conveys something of their shared capacity for playing. She recalls travelling in France and one night noticing crowds gathered to watch travelling acrobats; almost unnoticed, below them was "a little clown in a grey floppy coat, too big for him, just fooling around while the others did their display. Occasionally he made a fruitless attempt to jump up and reach at he bar. Then, suddenly, he made a great leap, and there he was, whirling around on the bar, all his clothes flying out, like a huge Catherine wheel, to roars of delight from the crowd. This is my image of Winnicott." Their shared delight in nonsense was important, she suggests, because playful nonsense is "the first phase of the creative process". She goes on to recall a *New Yorker* cartoon of two hippopotamuses, almost wholly immersed in the water: one is saying to the other, "I keep thinking it's Tuesday". She gave a copy to Winnicott, she says, and it became a joke that they shared. But characteristically, Marion turns the joke into a meditation on the area between land and water as an image of the threshold of consciousness, of the place where play—and creativity—becomes possible. Both she and Winnicott liked a line from Tagore, she recalls: "On the seashore of endless worlds children play." For herself, as for Winnicott, that line "aided speculation upon the question, If play is neither inside nor outside, where is it? For me, it stirred thoughts of the coming and going of the tides, the rhythmic daily submergence and smoothing out of this place where children play." She ends: "We must never try to make the hippo live only on land, because"—like herself, like Winnicott—"it is by nature incurably amphibious."

In the last years of life, Marion took great pleasure in coming to meetings of the *Squiggle* Foundation devoted to the study of Winnicott's work. She would turn up in Nina Farhi's sitting-room every Saturday morning, whatever the weather, whatever her state of health. Installed in the centre of the main sofa, she sometimes had difficulty in hearing everything the speaker said; she would nod off from time to time, make the occasional note, which often, later, she would need help in deciphering. But she was profoundly sustained by those Saturday mornings: in extreme old age, she had re-discovered a sense a community, a family almost, where she belonged, where everybody shared her interests, where she could make friends with people a quarter of her age.

In those years, Marion's failing sight prevented her from drawing or painting. But, with a creative ruthlessness characteristic of her, she took some of her own paintings—ones in which she had lost interest, that had somehow lost vitality for her—cut them up, and stuck them together in a series of collages. The collages vary in size—one is only about an inch square, others are larger; they are all superbly coloured—the colours sing, their contrasts lending depth and vitality to the shapes she is playing with. They used to hang on the wall opposite her armchair: she spent a lot of time talking and writing, free-associating, about the images. And there is a book still to come. In her 90s, Marion re-discovered the diaries she kept when her son was a baby and a small child, along with a little picture-book that he made at kindergarten. And, struggling with her failing sight, she began writing about them—-aiming, she said, at people who knew nothing about psychoanalysis. She called the new book—using a phrase from the child's storybook—*Bothered by Alligators*. It was, increasingly, about Marion herself, about her memories of her own childhood, about her sister, about

Winnicott, about all the people who had been important in her life, and, above all, about the meanings that she was discovering in the kindergarten picture book, and in her own collages. It had always been a moot point whether Marion was more at home working with images or with words; it was characteristic of her that she hedged her bets on that one till the very end.

CHAPTER TEN

Appreciations of Marion Milner

Dr Harold Stewart—psychoanalyst

I have known Marion ever since I was a student umpteen years ago. She was very a stylish person, very intelligent, and it was a pleasure to hear her speak at Scientific Meetings of the British Psycho-Analytical Society. In her last few years, she talked to me occasionally and sometimes invited me to come round to her house in Provost Road as there were certain Society affairs she wanted to discuss with me. A number of the things she said then were very sharp and very critical of some of her colleagues; she certainly wasn't wishy washy, although she could give that impression sometimes. Underneath, there was something much softer and gentler, although she clearly could be quite firm. I am sure that if you are the sister of a Nobel Prize winner, you have to do something to hold your end up.

Her writings, at least some of them, were very useful to me, particularly *The Hands of the Living God*. When I first read it, I was astonished by its contents as it was so completely different from the usual emphasis on transference and countertransference, and verbal behaviour. Her use of her patient's drawings expanded my own mental horizon, and I valued that enormously. I particularly found it useful when I came across such patients myself; there were certain problems they were having, and I found that her book was illuminating for me. One of these patients was a borderline hallucinating hysteric, whose ways of acting out her regressive features was to produce paintings and drawings, some very similar to the ones produced by Marion's patient. I certainly thought after a time that my patient must have read *The Hands of the Living God*, and she was quite honest and said that she had. Nevertheless, she had her own variations of what was going on in her own mind, and some of the things she was producing were quite works of art in their own right. They illustrated rather different material from that produced by Marion's patient, and it was interesting to explore it. I am not an artist, and I certainly did not have Marion's feel for what art conveyed to her and what it might mean intrapsychically. I am much more prosaic, so the only way I could investigate it was by a sort of free-associative technique, treating it rather like a dream, and this proved useful to both of us.

I also found the book a help when I was trying to conceptualize various states of inner emptiness that had been experienced by another patient, similar in some ways to Susan but this time without the drawings. Marion's description of the physical bases of inner emptiness was very pertinent to me, particularly as there is little in the literature on inner emptiness. I think that painting as a physical activity must have been a great help to Marion in her researches into these primitive psycho-physical areas, and I do value them. She was a great lady.

Dr Peter Bruggen—retired consultant psychiatrist and author

After a meeting with the Training Secretary of the Institute of Psycho-Analysis (I had been hauled over the coals for my attitude), I received a letter. It told me that, although I was to be allowed to continue my psychoanalytic training, my first supervisor had to be a man. Marion Milner was my analyst, and she suggested Winnicott. I wrote to him and he agreed. Some few weeks before we started, we passed on the Institute stairs and I introduced myself. He screwed up his eyes and said: "I look forward to discussing a case with you." It was a shockingly delightful definition of the relationship he anticipated: he was not into being hierarchical and was not going to be telling me what to do.

When I started my supervision, I found the experience to be marvellous. Winnicott was exhilarating and infuriating. He was so unstructured that he was happy to discuss other matters besides my training case (though he helped with that too!). I had recently become a consultant psychiatrist at an adolescent unit where some of the policies we introduced became controversial. His supervision then was immensely valuable.

He had told me that when I arrived I should open the unlocked front door and go in. One week when I did this, I found him asleep on the floor. He had told me what to do if that happened, and I did it: I woke him.

On the following week, a few hours before I was to set off for my supervision, I was handed a note. His secretary had phoned to cancel my appointment because Dr Winnicott had died. It seemed a joke (cancelled because he had died), yet carried a message I had dreaded, for I knew how ill he had been. It filled me with grief.

At eight the following morning, I had my analytic session. I rang the bell and had the usual seemingly long wait as Marion Milner came along the corridor to open the door. I was shocked by what I saw, but entered, walked as usual to her room, and lay on the couch. When she had sat down, I said: "You looked so sad."

I have thought of all the things an analyst could do with those words. How transference and projection could be interpreted. All she said was: "So did you." I know that during that session we were both crying.

It was international news that came into my mind on another day. Part way through the session, I said: "And Martin Luther King has been killed." Again, I have thought of all that an analyst could make of that. She said: "Yes."

I think those two statements were among the most valuable things that I got from Marion Milner. We were sharing journeys in a world with pain. But there were things we could do to make it more bearable and more fun. She helped me with that.

Mike Brearley—psychoanalyst

Like Margaret Walters, I too have read *A Life of One's Own*, without knowing anything about psychoanalysis at all—well, hardly anything. It was the first personal account in this field that I had read. I got the blue-and-white paperback and read it backwards and around, and I also looked at the photograph. I remember being on a train after giving a talk to a Workers' Educational Meeting in Luton. Coming back on the train, a desolate empty train, into London, I remember ruminating over this picture, and my feeling was different to Margaret's: I thought she was beautiful, and I fell rather in love with her, not only from what she said but from this picture.

Some years after that, I started to get interested in the idea of training or becoming a therapist or analyst or I don't know what—anyway, training in this area and getting involved. And I went to see Marion Milner, and the way it turned out was this: that someone was pursuing me at that time, a public figure. A woman was pursuing me, not I think in other ways, she was pursuing me just to have dinner with her. I thought that she was not a woman I wanted to have dinner with, and I kept trying to keep her off. She was a very persistent woman, and her last throw was to say that if she could get anyone in London that I chose to come to this dinner, would I come? And I said, thinking what the hell: Marion Milner. And she got her. As you see, Marion would be immediately game for anything. She was curious about life, amused, wondering what she was going to, but actually looking forward to it. So she and I went off to dinner, a very tedious dinner I remember, except the only good thing about it was there was someone who had sailed around the world. I remember we were both fascinated by this, and afterwards I went to see her and said that I am going to try to train, I am in the process of making applications to train—and would she be my analyst. It was this picture again! She said that she couldn't because she was too old. She recommended Pearl King. I went to Pearl King in the end, but what Marion said then was that she had a question for me. Her grandson was very proud of something he had done at school and she didn't know what this thing was. And this thing was a hat trick. Please would I please explain what a hat trick was.

That must have been in the early to mid-1970s, and many years after that we moved into the same street as Marion and I got to know her on a regular basis and she got to know our family; she would come, at the age of 85 or 90 and sit on the stairs talking to our small children—they were smallish then—and being really curious and interested, and, as Margaret said, always being rather elegant and beautiful. My wife, who is Indian, used to bring silk shirts from India for her, and she would wear nice Indian-type scarves. One day when she was in her 90s, we had lunch in the garden; we had a long swing hanging from a tree, and she said she hadn't been on a swing for sixty years, and could she have a go on the swing. All of these things that are so wonderful and curious and loveable.

Later even than that, she always had an admiration and a curiosity for current analysis and analysts and what she thought she had missed. And although she wrote a book about the destructive element, she was quite aware of things that she thought she had missed, both in her analysis with Winnicott and in her previous analysis, about the extent of her anger or cruelty or violence. She thought that was always missing. She was of a very analytic orientation and would interpret anything in her body as having an unconscious element, often of aggression. She got a burst blood-vessel in her eye, which she said must have been to do with her own aggression that she hadn't been able to understand. I think I'll stop there.

Val Richards—former Assistant Director, Squiggle

Marion's magisterial paper, "The Role of Illusion in Symbol Formation", has already been discussed here and anything I wanted to say about it has very much been said. One thing that has not been pointed out, however, is that the boy in that paper was Melanie Klein's grandson, and Klein was supervising Marion for that case as well. Although she did not remember what she had written in that paper she did remember this point, and I think that that is what makes remarkable her refusal to be guided by the theoretical concerns that were imposed upon her and, instead, to simply be open to the meaning of the boy's playing. This was all the more courageous. The other thing I really want to say is that what strikes me in my fairly limited experience of Marion is that meaning had a greater priority for her above fact, above theory. And it seemed to me that in *The Hands of the Living God* a big factor in the duration of the analysis was Susan's instinctive reliance on Marion's certainty to be grabbed by those drawings in the conviction that they would yield a "true" meaning. Even more striking, I cannot help wondering if her long life was to do with the way in which she had faith and belief that it was possible to arrive at the true meaning—or *a* true meaning—of experience, as if she was scared of what we might call the post-modernist slippage of meaning that we are probably all prey to.

The last time I saw her, and as I know happened with many of us, I received a summons from her, to see her in hospital after she'd had a bad fall. I did not dread this visit, because I knew there would not be any tricky small talk, as she always asked you to come for a reason. On this occasion, she asked me to check a point about Winnicott. It was something in his paper "Fear of Breakdown". The night before her fall she had had two dreams, which she told me about in great detail and then said with tremendous urgency: "Now could that be what Winnicott meant about the fear of breakdown?" It was as if everything depended on the validation of this point. She was made secure by the belief that you could get hold of the truth. It was true that she desperately minded not having her anger analysed by Winnicott, and in fact I think she was terribly angry about this. At least her anger did come out, and at the age of 97—I don't know if others can corroborate this—she was contemplating going to see a therapist about it.

Amelie Noack—former Assistant Director, Squiggle

I met Marion originally when collecting her from home and driving her to and from Nina Fahri's. When Nina told me she had selected me for that honour, I felt hesitant and thought: "I will have to leave twenty minutes earlier than usual and I will be back later." But from the first time I collected Marion, it was absolutely amazing. During our shared journey, we talked and these talks were—I can only call them creative, because something happened between Marion and me. We talked normally during those talks, but it seemed to me we were travelling through the history of psychoanalysis, in the fifteen minutes there and fifteen minutes back. The seminar time in between didn't seem to matter; it got integrated into our discussion. There seemed to be this stream of material and history that went on between us. On one of these journeys, she told me she was working on a book based on the picture book that John had made when he was 4 years old. She told me the story, which I couldn't understand at the time, but John was upset and had said, "I think you must be troubled by alligators", and she wanted to use this as the title. I couldn't really understand what she was saying, but on another level it seemed to make perfect sense. That is one thing that I learned from Marion for which I am immensely grateful, because I think I learned something about doing analysis and having analysis that I have not had with any of the other analysts in my life.

The other thing that happened was that Marion would invite people to come to spend an hour or 50 minutes with her, and during those talks we started to talk about poetry. One of the poets I find especially important is Rilke, and Marion told me that she analysed one of the English translators of the *Duino Elegies*. She said she could never make sense of Rilke's poetry, and I made up my mind that this would have to change and I would somehow have to help her understand him. So I brought my German/English Rilke to a meeting and tried to read—actually did read—those parts that I find especially moving. I tried to put all my understanding of the German language into the translation—and I didn't get anywhere. I couldn't help her understand Rilke. I think that's how I want to leave it.

Dr. Barnett—psychoanalyst and friend

I want to share a very brief vignette. Marion Milner was the person I went to as my second consultant for the full membership course of the British Psycho-Analytical Society. It was an extraordinary experience of something that hasn't been mentioned—well, perhaps it has been: it has certainly been implied. It was the experience of being in her presence. I went to her every month for these consultations, and she said very little; it was quite extraordinary but there was something in her presence that said a great deal about the material I was presenting. One day I told her that my patient had brought a dream to me. I was a very serious and earnest, even a pompous kind of student, and very much in awe of Marion Milner, and so I was very po-faced and told her my patient's dream: he was piloting an aeroplane and had his hand on the joystick, and the joystick turned into a banana. Marion laughed and I saw the joke, but I hadn't seen it before. That was, really, the essence of the supervision. It is something I will never forget, because it helped me to be less serious, less pompous, able to think about a patient who might want to share a joke with me. Really, almost a joke on psychoanalysis as well as on me. She was a wonderful person to go to for consultation.

Andrew Cockburn—psychiatrist and psychotherapist

These stories about Marion have been reviving memories for me. About ten years ago I had written a paper on what William Blake meant to me as a psychotherapist and I was having a lot of trouble getting it published. It was turned down all over the place, and I was talking to a colleague—I think it was Andrea Sabbadini—who said I should speak to Marion Milner. I rather quaked when she said that because, although I was familiar with some of her books and articles, I had never met her. So I can remember sitting in front of the telephone for about twenty minutes trying to pluck up the courage to dial, and then saying: "You don't know me but it has been suggested I contact you about this paper." And she said in a very clipped professional voice, "Right, bring it round", and down went the phone. Fortunately, she lived just around the corner. She took the paper, said "Hello", and the door shut. And three days later there was a phone call, and she said: "I think it's absolutely delightful and I think it should be published in the Winnicott journal, and come and see me." And so I did, and we had a long talk and that led to her saying: "See my friend Nina and have a word with her." I had been a member of *Squiggle* when it first started, but my membership had dropped off. I rejoined and turned up for the Saturday morning seminars at Nina's and had the privilege for a whole year of taking Marion there and back. We became great friends, and I received many invitations to come and see her, nearly always to talk about William Blake. The last was only five days before she died. I remember going in, and the only difference I noticed—and it struck me deeply—was that Marion did not rise, it was the first time she had not stood up, and I had a qualm. Anyway, it was a transforming experience.

Anonymous

I would like to speak about Marion as a neighbour. I first met her when I moved into this locality and joined The *Squiggle* in the mid-1980s, which were also her middle 80s. She taught me a lot about how to start a new garden. She was still crazy about gardening and very much resented having to have a man do the heavier work. As much as possible she did it herself. We used to run into each other and give each other tips. She once had a problem with dry rot in the ceiling of her lavatory and asked me what to do, and I sent her round a man who was very reliable and honest. He told her what to do and told her she didn't need a specialist but an ordinary builder, and he refused to take a fee. She gave him a cup of tea. He sat down on the floor of her sitting-room and poured out his troubles to her for a couple of hours. Anyway, he got two hours of first-class counselling, and they were both really very pleased with the encounter.

We were very proud about the two superb hens on her wall. I once asked her, after there had been a play about Melanie Klein, whether Melanie Klein was really like that, and she said: "Oh yes—as a matter of fact, her most frequent interpretation of just about anything a child could produce was, 'Ah yes, zat is ze excrement of the mother'."

Finally, one of her less successful patients was a chap who was referred to her and who, she realized very soon, was totally unsuitable for psychotherapy—indeed, any form of therapy—because he had absolutely no feelings. She told him this and advised him to go off and live his life some other way, but he refused. She refused to take him on as a psychotherapeutic patient but he refused to leave, so they compromised that he would come every now and again and just have a chat with her. This went on for years and years and years until she was in her early 90s. She said: "Now look, you really must stop. How would you feel if I were to die when you were still my patient?" He thought for a very long time, and said: "Bereft." And she was quite chuffed, as this was the first sign of feeling he had ever shown.

Martina Thompson—art therapist, author, long-standing friend

Marion Milner was Honorary President of the British Association of Art Therapists (BAAT) from the late 1970s until her death. By the time I came to know her in the late 1980s, she had ceased being involved in BAAT matters, but it was obvious that she always retained a special welcome for art therapists. Marion lived, above all, by images. Images were her sustenance—images she had made (or that had made themselves, as she might have said) in paint or clay, images from dreams, from memories, those thrown up by an "interior vagabondage", from myths, from the Bible, from poetry. Things vividly seen and held as pictures in the mind, like the poisonous centipede first met in a dream and then startlingly confronted in the zoo, which she wrote about in *An Experiment in Leisure.* She would occupy herself again and again with these images, hover over them, perceive new things in them, make new connections. She had, after all, wanted to be a naturalist, and the nature diary she kept as a child of 11 has the most delicate watercolour drawings, all acutely observed. She seemed to have retained this quality of seeing. Her perusal of Blake's drawings for the Book of Job made her see things that I doubt any art historian ever noticed; for instance, that at the beginning Job's face is the same as God's. It gave rise to a wonderful piece of writing, *The Sense in Non-Sense,* where she paralleled Blake's perceptions with those of psychoanalysis.

At one time, Marion would keep presenting her friends with a somewhat disturbing, rapidly done charcoal sketch, one of several such by D. W. Winnicott, who had been a close colleague and briefly her analyst. It was of a mother holding a baby—and, what, she would ask, did they make of it? One friend got fed up with this: "You repeat yourself, Marion," she said, "you're a gramophone record." But she wasn't. There was always a shift. She had a way of emptying her mind of any preconceptions. Her unconscious, like Balaam's ass, would let her know what's what, even if it hadn't the words to tell her. A bit like living on the countertransference. She very much regretted that the countertransference had to be kept in check in her days as a practising analyst.

Her books are a bit like detective stories, where by looking she is led from clue to clue, further and further into the plot, always alert, poised, and ready. At all times she found clues in her own body—that is, when she could achieve muscular relaxation and allow herself to "sink down" into it without interfering thoughts. Then it proved indeed a "big sagacity". "My sole concern was", she wrote, "to borrow forms, no matter from where, by which my own preoccupations could declare themselves."

And as she could use the same pregnant, potent images again and again in this way, I considered that, while we nowadays are extravagantly after the new, she was most economical. I told her that she was the arch-recycler. When I first met Marion Milner—and it was because of my book—she took me into a light, spacious room. "Would you like some tea?" she asked, "Or some whisky?" "Whisky, I think", I said. "Good", she said smiling openly, and we never looked back. At the many meetings that followed, the bottle of Teacher's, the jug of water, and two tiny glasses were ritual. At that time, Marion still had a patient who gave her "a lot to think about". But soon she hoped to paint. In the meantime, she was recycling old discarded paintings, cutting out pieces that she liked and playing with them till they settled in satisfactory positions. In her beloved studio room, there were always two or three of these collages-in-process laid out on trays or boards and balanced on various piles of books. One day, with the idea of sorting out her affairs, she went on an archaeological dig in the bog of her papers (her words) and lifted out a story book written at school by her son. She also came across a diary she had kept from the time he was 2 years old. These two things posed so many questions that she found she had the substance of her last book on her hands.

Eventually she had to give up her upper room to two young people, who would be there for her if she needed them. She settled into her consulting room bringing her collages—now framed—with her and also some six or eight small clay heads she had made.

The collages, about twenty of them, with names like *Wobegone, The Listeners*, and *She Thought He Was the Gardener*, were together on one wall; the clay heads—*The Singing Rabbi* and *Sad Mr. Freud* among them—stood opposite on the mantelpiece. These were her witnesses and were often consulted. From that time on, she would sit in what she came to call her social chair, a chair draped in yellow, set about with more and more anglepoise lamps the more blind she became.

As time went on and the book grew, and as Matthew, a young painter who had come to clean the house, was duly diverted into typing it on the word processor, little heaps of manuscript grew all around. "I think you'll find the bit I want you to read in the second pile from the window. Or it's on top of that end lot on the couch. . . ." This became the routine for all her more regular visitors.

She had a mischievous, wicked smile, beautiful, vibrant, humorous. She loved words and the shape of sentences, she told me, even more than paint. But imagine what a task she had: her eyes, so bad she couldn't make out her own writing. If she dropped pages, she couldn't pick them up. Often low in mood, it was a struggle for her; but the book led her on. It was an inspiration to watch her.

The last time I saw her, she was in her bedroom, a dark room at garden level, cluttered with baskets and gardening tools and all sorts of stuff. She was sitting bolt upright on the edge of her bed, terribly agitated, terribly distressed. Her cheeks were wet with tears when I kissed her. Within this distress, or out of it, she found the last line for her difficult Winnicott chapter and told me it. By seven o'clock she was somewhat comforted and, fiercely independent, ready for me to go. That night she died.

REFERENCES

Amelio, G. (1995). Bertolucci secondo il cinema. In: *Gianni Amelio* (pp. 99–100), ed. G. Volpi. Turin: Edizioni Scriptorium.

Bate, W. J. (1963). *John Keats.* Cambridge, MA: Harvard University Press.

Bell, C. (1914). *Art.* Oxford: Oxford University Press.

Bollas, C. (1987). *The Shadow of the Object—Psychoanalysis of the Unthought Known.* London: Free Association Books.

Bollas, C. (1989). *Forces of Destiny.* London: Free Association Books.

Bloom, H. (1994). *The Western Canon: The Books and School of the Ages.* London: Macmillan

Bonaminio, V., & Di Renzo, M. (1996). Giocare e sognare come potenziali esperienze complete del Sé. Senso e non-senso nel materiale clinico della relazione analitica con bambini e adolescenti. *Richard e Piggle, 4*: 9–22.

Britton, R. (1998). *Belief and Imagination: Explorations in Psychoanalysis.* London: Routledge.

Carroll, L. (1865). *Alice's Adventures in Wonderland.* In: *The Annotated Alice. Alice's Adventures in Wonderland and Through the Looking-Glass.* Harmondsworth: Penguin Books.

Chatwin, B. (1987). *The Songlines.* London: Picador.

Eliot, T. S. (1951). Philip Massinger. In: *Selected Essays* (pp. 205–220). London: Faber & Faber.

Ferro, A. (1992). *La tecnica della psicoanalisi infantile.* Milan: Cortina.

Freud, E. L. (Ed.) (1970). *The Letters of Sigmund Freud and Arnold Zweig.* London: Hogarth Press.

Freud, S. (1900a). *The Interpretation of Dreams. S.E., 4–5.*

Freud, S. (1905c). *Jokes and Their Relation to the Unconscious. S.E., 8.*

Freud, S. (1905d). *Three Essays on the Theory of Sexuality. S.E., 7.*

Freud, S. (1908e [1907]). Creative writers and day-dreaming. *S.E., 9.*

Freud, S. (1910c). *Leonardo da Vinci and a Memory of His Childhood. S.E., 11.*

Freud, S. (1920g). *Beyond the Pleasure Principle. S.E., 18.*

Freud, S. (1928b). Dostoevsky and parricide. *S.E., 21.*

Freud, S. (1930a). *Civilization and Its Discontents. S.E., 21.*

Freud, S. (1942a [1905–6]). Psychopathic characters on the stage. *S.E., 7.*

Fry, R. (1924). *The Artist and Psychoanalysis.* London: Hogarth Press.

Giannakoulas, A. (1992). *Introduzione all'edizione italiana di M. Milner, La follia rimossa delle persone sane.* Rome: Armando.

Green, A. (1983). The dead mother. In: *On Private Madness.* London: Hogarth Press, 1986.

Green, A. (1997). The intuition of the negative in *Playing and Reality. International Journal of Psycho-Analysis, 78*: 1071–1084.

Greenacre, P. (1957). The childhood of the artist: libidinal development and giftedness. *Psychoanalytic Study of the Child,* 12: 27–72.

Hernandez, M., & Giannakoulas, A. (1997). "Sulla costruzione dello spazio potenziale." Paper presented at the International Congress on the Psychesoma, Milan, April.

Jones, E. (1949). *Hamlet and Oedipus.* London: Victor Gollancz.

Khan, M. (1958). Introduction. *Through Paediatrics to Psychoanalysis.* London: Hogarth Press, 1987.

Khan, M. (1962). Dream psychology and the evolution of the psychoanalytic situation. In: *The Privacy of the Self.* London: Hogarth Press, 1974.

Khan, M. (1972). The use and abuse of dream in psychic experience. In: *The Privacy of the Self.* London: Hogarth Press, 1974.

Khan, M. (1976). Beyond the dreaming experience. In: *Hidden Selves.* London: Hogarth Press, 1983.

Khan, M. (1979). *Lo spazio privato del Sé.* Torino: Boringhieri.

Langer, S. (1942). *Philosophy in a New Key.* Cambridge, MA: Harvard University Press.

Langer, S. (1953). *Feeling and Form.* London: Routledge & Kegan Paul.

Laplanche, J. (1976). *Life and Death in Psychoanalysis.* Johns Hopkins University Press, paperback edition 1985.

Lear, J. (1990). *Love and Its Place in Nature.* New York: Farrar, Straus & Giroux [reprinted by Yale University Press, 1998].

Mahler, M., Pine, F., & Bergman, A. (1975). *The Psychological Birth of the Human Infant.* London: Hutchinson.

Meltzer, D. (1983). *Dream-Life: A Re-examination of Psycho-Analytical Theory and Technique.* Reading: Clunie Press.

Merleau-Ponty, M. (1964). Indirect language and the voices of silence. In: *Signs,* trans. R. McCleary. Evanston, IL: Northwestern University Press.

Milner, M. [J. Field, pseud.] (1934). *A Life of One's Own.* London: Virago, 1986.

Milner, M. (1942). The child's capacity for doubt. In: *The Suppressed Madness of Sane Men* (pp. 12–15). London: Tavistock, 1987.

Milner, M. [J. Field, pseud.] (1950). *On Not Being Able to Paint,* 2nd ed. London: Heineman, 1981.

Milner, M. (1952a). The framed gap. In: *The Suppressed Madness of Sane Men* (pp. 79–83). London: Tavistock, 1987.

Milner, M. (1952b). The role of illusion in symbol formation. In: *The Suppressed Madness of Sane Men* (pp. 83–113). London: Tavistock, 1987.

Milner, M. (1957). The ordering of chaos. In: *The Suppressed Madness of Sane Men* (pp. 216–233). London: Tavistock, 1987.

Milner, M. (1972). Winnicott and the two way journey. In: *The Suppressed Madness of Sane Men* (pp. 246–252). London: Tavistock, 1987.

Milner, M. (1975). A discussion of Masud Khan's paper "In Search of the Dreaming Experience". In: *The Suppressed Madness of Sane Men* (pp. 275–278). London: Tavistock, 1987.

Milner, M. (1977). Winnicott and overlapping circles. In: *The Suppressed Madness of Sane Men* (pp. 287–298). London: Tavistock, 1987.

Milner, M. (1986). *An Experiment in Leisure.* London: Virago.

Milner, M (1987a). *Eternity's Sunrise.* London: Virago.

Milner, M. (1987b). *The Suppressed Madness of Sane Men.* London: Tavistock.

Milner, M. (1988). *The Hands of the Living God.* London: Virago

Podro, M. (1998). *Depiction.* New Haven, CT/London: Yale University Press.

Podro, M. (1999). Review of *Rembrandt by Himself. Burlington Magazine,* September, pp. 553–556.

Proust, M. (1923). *The Captive.* In: *In Search of Lost Time,* trans. C. Scott Moncrieff, T. Kilmartin, & D. J. Enright. London: Chatto & Windus, 1992.

Raupp, H.-J. (1984). *Untersuchungen zu Kiinsterldarstellung in den Nederlanden im 17. Jahrhundert.* Olms: Hildersheim.

Rilke, R. M. (1960). *Selected Works, Vol. 2: Poetry,* trans. J. B. Leishman. London: Hogarth Press.

Rilke, R.M. (1966). *Ausgewehlte Gedichte.* Frankfurt am Main: Suhrkamp.

Segal, H. (1957). Notes on symbol formation. In: *The Work of Hannah Segal: A Kleinian Approach to Clinical Practice* (pp. 49–65). London: Free Association Books, 1986.

Segal, H. (1991). *Dream, Phantasy, Art.* London: Routledge.

Sharpe, E. F. (1929). The impatience of Hamlet. In: *Collected Papers on Psychoanalysis* (pp. 203–213). London: Hogarth Press, 1978.

Sharpe, E. F. (1937). *Dream Analysis.* London: Hogarth Press.

Stern, D. (1985). *The Interpersonal World of the Infant.* New York: Basic Books.

Trevarthen, C. (1993). Playing into reality: conversations with the infant communicator. *Winnicott Studies,* 7 (Spring).

White, C., & Buvelot, Q. (1999). *Rembrandt by Himself.* London: National Gallery Publications; The Hague: Royal Cabinet of Paintings, Mauritshuis.

Wilson, J. D. (1951). *What Happens in Hamlet.* Cambridge: Cambridge University Press

Winnicott, C. (1989). D.W.W.: a reflection. In: D. W. Winnicott, *Psycho-Analytic Explorations,* ed. R. Shepherd, C. Winnicott, & M. Davis. London: Karnac Books.

Winnicott, D. W. (1941). The observation of infants in a set situation. In: *Through Paediatrics to Psycho-Analysis.* London: Hogarth Press, 1975. [Reprinted London: Karnac Books, 1992.]

Winnicott, D. W. (1945). Primitive emotional development. In: *Through Paediatrics to Psycho-Analysis* (pp. 145–156). London: Hogarth Press, 1975. [Reprinted London: Karnac Books, 1992.]

Winnicott, D. W. (1951). Transitional objects and transitional phenomena. In: *Through Paediatrics to Psycho-Analysis* (pp. 229–242). London: Hogarth Press, 1975. [Reprinted London: Karnac Books, 1992.] Also in: *Playing and Reality* (pp. 1–25). London: Tavistock, 1971.

Winnicott D. W. (1953). (Review of) *Psychoanalytic Studies of the Personality* by W. R. D. Fairbairn. *International Journal of Psycho-Analysis, 34.*

Winnicott, D. W. (1958). *Collected Papers: Through Paediatrics to Psycho-analysis.* London: Tavistock. [Reprinted as *Through Paediatrics to Psycho-Analysis.* London: Hogarth Press, 1975; reprinted London: Karnac Books, 1992.]

Winnicott, D. W. (1965). *The Maturational Processes and the Facilitating Environment.* London: Hogarth Press. [Reprinted London: Karnac Books, 1990.]

Winnicott, D. W. (1966). On the split off male and female elements. In: *Psycho-Analytic Explorations* (pp 163–192), ed. C. Winnicott, R. Shepherd, & M. Davis. London: Karnac Books, 1989.

Winnicott, D. W. (1967). The location of cultural experience. In: *Playing and Reality* (pp. 95–103). London: Tavistock, 1971.

Winnicott, D. W. (1968a). Playing and culture. In: *Psycho-Analytic Explorations* (pp. 203–206), ed. R. Shepherd, C. Winnicott, & M. Davis. London: Karnac Books.

Winnicott, D. W. (1968b). The use of an object and relating through identifications. In: *Psycho-Analytic Explorations* (pp. 218–227), ed. R. Shepherd, C. Winnicott, & M. Davis. London: Karnac Books.

Winnicott, D. W. (1969). Comments on my paper "The Use of an Object". In: *Psycho-Analytic Explorations* (pp. 239–240), ed. R. Shepherd, C. Winnicott, & M. Davis. London: Karnac Books.

Winnicott, D. W. (1971a). Mirror role of mother and family in child development. In: *Playing and Reality* (pp. 111–118). London: Tavistock, 1971.

Winnicott, D. W. (1971b). Playing: a theoretical statement. In: *Playing and reality* (pp. 38–52). London: Tavistock Publications.

Winnicott, D. W. (1986). *Home Is Where We Start From.* London: Penguin.

Winnicott, D. W. (1989). *Psycho-Analytic Explorations*, ed. R. Shepherd, C. Winnicott, & M. Davis. London: Karnac Books.

Winnicott, D. W. (1996). *Thinking about Children*, ed. R. Shepherd, J. Johns, & H. Taylor Robinson. London: Karnac Books.

Winnicott, D. W. (n.d). Knowing and not-knowing: a clinical example. In: *Psycho-Analytic Explorations* (pp. 24–25), ed. R. Shepherd, C. Winnicott, & M. Davis. London: Karnac Books.

Wright, K. (1991). *Vision and Separation: Between Mother and Baby*. London: Free Association Books.

Woolf, V. (1941). *Between the Acts*, ed. F. Kermode. Oxford: Oxford University Press, 1992.

INDEX